A BOOK OF CELEBRATIONS

Books by the same author
A Book of Festivals
A Book of Projects
Creative Work with Found Materials

A Book of Celebrations

DEREK WATERS

MILLS & BOON LIMITED, LONDON

First published in Great Britain 1971 by
Mills and Boon Limited, 17–19 Foley Street, London WIA IDR

ISBN 0 263.51673.3

Made and printed by Oxley Press Ltd., Edinburgh.
All orders and enquiries should be sent to the publishers (address at
top of page) and not to the printer.

CONTENTS

ACKNOWLEDGEMENTS

I should like to thank Joan Bryant for her enthusiastic interest, encouragement and practical advice with this book of celebrations; David Clarke, Pageant Master of the 1968 Guildford Celebrations for information about this particular form of artistic creation; Mansel Connick, Headmaster of All Souls School, Foley Street, London, for the opportunity to watch his Midsummer Festival in which he involved his whole school, of whom 60 per cent were from many different cultures and traditions; Mary Wilson, until her retirement Headmistress of Redriffe School in Rotherhithe, for her valuable advice on organisation and the chance to see her Festival of Singing Games; Ralph Lavender for assistance in compiling the data for an historical pageant — The Norman Invasion; Pamela Hill for children's work linked with the Easter Celebration; Esme Waters, Margaret Brandham and John Bailey for assistance with certain musical items.

All other staff, past and present, of Boxgrove School for their enthusiastic involvement, co-operation, interest and varying interpretations of the various themes; the children of Boxgrove School, past and present, some thousand in number, with experience in many cases of twenty celebrations, for the way in which they showed that they could respond to this kind of stimulus and enjoy themselves.

Alec Davis for his illustrative interpretations of each of the celebrations, and Mrs. Greta Kinder and Timothy Waters for the drawings in support of the art and craft suggestions.

D.W.

A CASE FOR CELEBRATIONS

I think that as a nation we are in danger of losing the art of congregation in which there is any sense of participation. Many of our churches stand empty and it needs a needle match such as Chelsea versus Leeds before the terraces are full! On less auspicious football occasions, the greatest pleasure appears to come from the abuse of the referee or the damage that can be inflicted on railway carriages.

Agencies are at work to eliminate religious assemblies in school, and when one sees and hears what is perpetrated in the name of God, one can feel a certain sympathy with their views! Perhaps we need to remind ourselves that it is the content of the programme that they wish to change, not the act of assembly. This volume of protest has had a valuable reaction amongst Christians; they too have looked searchingly at their own practices and many newer and more exciting assemblies have been created.

Part of the problem is lack of opportunity. Britain has a mere six national holidays a year, and only the People's Republic of China has fewer. Italy has sixteen public holidays, Sweden sixteen and a half and the Virgin Isles twenty-one. One of these celebrates Roosevelt's birthday and another is called Organic Act Day, whatever that could be. I saw a young lady the other day wearing one of those bright lapel badges which read 'I AM A VIRGIN islander'. I know now what she was smiling about — all her many opportunities to celebrate.

Spain, which has been subject to many invasions, and where there is a close alliance between the State and the Church, has a large calendar of regional festivities. From such a diverse pattern of ideologies and cultures, an extraordinary mixture of pagan and religious festivals results. You may well feel you would prefer to miss the Festival of Puebla del Caraminal, when those who feel death approaching, walk through the town shrouded in white, trailed by next of kin carrying coffins.

However, most celebrations are joyful occasions, and frequent.
In Northern Greece, for instance, there seems to be a saint to celebrate once a fortnight, and in most Roman Catholic countries there are numerous and often unexpected festivals, as anyone will know who has tried to shop in Italy. Whether the recent purging of saints such as St. Nicholas and St. Christopher will lead to a decline in the amount of sacred punctuation of the year remains to be seen.

What is interesting to note is that in many of the countries listed, there is poverty amongst a large proportion of the population and yet (or perhaps we might say because of it) festivals take place. However hard pressed, they always find a cause for rejoicing. It is as though the dead saint has come alive again and the populace wants to show that it is alive too. With careless abandon everyone is taken up by the Festival and ordinary life is put aside. With work and sometimes domestic affairs so tedious, it is small wonder that such people enjoy their festivals.

It was so in the Britain of long ago too. Festivals were a time of revelry and renewal, when life was seen in a wider perspective, but whenever the ecclesiastical authorities saw these forms of native expression, they denounced them. Dancing in church had to stop, and in its place a more sober holy joy was encouraged. In their infinite wisdom, since they could not prohibit everything they interpreted as the work of the devil, they integrated some of the practices within the Christian calendar. So the great Roman Feast of Saturnalia and the Calends of the Winter Solstice were merged with the Holy Celebration of Christmas. Still centuries afterwards, holly and ivy, tribal symbols of sexual rituals, are used for decorations in December in many households and churches. Mistletoe has long been connected with Druid worship and yet it is a symbol, at least tolerated by the Church.

The carols we sing with great gusto at Christmas – and more frequently now at other times of the year – underline this need to celebrate in an almost spontaneous way. It is a pleasure to hear and watch the Lord of the Dance (Galliard Ltd.) sung and danced at Christmas and Easter. In the last two decades, there has been a great increase in the number of festivals which have been held in this country. Many cities, and not a few towns mount a programme over a few days or weeks and attract many visitors as well as their own inhabitants. Often a particular type of festival becomes associated with a certain town, and those who come to join in the festivities know what to expect. Edinburgh, in spite of being so large, has this distinct character, and so has Aldeburgh. But perhaps it is at the Wexford Festival that one feels that an almost perfect shape has emerged with the town and tourists, and the events all coming together in delightful combination. As well as features which make up the main personality of the festival, fringe activities cluster around some centres. A 'Psychedelic Evening' was included at Spoleto recently; wrestling, rather surprisingly, at Cheltenham, and at Belfast there was a 'Cook-In': so perhaps we can almost say that when celebrating, anything goes.

One always hopes to be original in one's choice of festival, and quite often one is, in the interpretation of the idea. So it is quite a good idea to keep one's eyes and mind open and look at various Calendars of Events, e.g. in *The Times* and *Observer* newspapers in the spring when the plans have been announced for the great Festivals of Europe and beyond. One might come across a reference to the Nasrudin Festival. This is the annual Turkish celebration in the town of Eskishehr which is the reputed birthplace of that incomparable fellow — Mulla Nasrudin. Idries Shah has retold many of the amazing exploits of the Mulla (Cape) and many of these tales are suitable for improvisation. Could a writer from these islands become a suitable case for treatment?

Perhaps an item of news that there was a Festival of Bread at Myrddin in Carmarthenshire, in which there were 365 different kinds of loaves on show, could set the mind working on how this could be adapted to make just a small change in the annual Harvest Festival, which is so far removed from the urban child's experience today. Might the reference to a seafood supper held on May 3rd in Rhoose, Glamorganshire, to celebrate Captain O'Neale's attack and repulsion at Llanwit, make one curious to discover whether your town has ever heard a shot fired in anger? While researching into the history of wool, will the information that St. George was Patron Saint of the Shepherds, St. James for the Weavers, and St. Blaise for the woolcombers, suggest a variation of approach with children which could include drama, singing and dancing? Is there a fair (or was there one) granted by charter as at Leyburn by Richard II, or at Easingwold (also in Yorkshire) where in 1291 Edward 1st granted the town the right to hold an annual market in September, and named it the Market of the Vigil and Feast of the Nativity of the Blessed Virgin Mary, and could the school in some way participate in the occasion or try to recreate it?

One might even wonder when looking in on the television reports of party conferences each year, just how their activities fit in with ancient tribal rituals. Attacks on the Opposition are virulent, and each sally is loudly cheered by the members, especially when the headman is being insulted. The camera at such moments lets us see the arm-waving of the men and the waving head-dresses of their women. Then we have the presentation of the leader, and loud and long are the cheers and hopes for success in the approaching conflict. A Festival of Politics perhaps?

From the examples already given, and other themes which will be suggested later in the book, it is clear that there are many occasions when some organised form of celebration could take place. The important question is whether such festivals have any place in school.

In writing a book for teachers, the author is at risk, because of the jargon and clichés which he may use. Labels and definitions may seem apt but are they rather too superficial? So it is rather difficult to describe in concrete terms just what one hopes to achieve in the educational process with each child. Certainly one wishes each child to belong to and make a contribution to the group of which he is a member. In suggesting larger formations for these events of celebration, I would want each child to participate not only in the work of one class, but also the larger body of the school. This would not be a vague contribution but rather a definite act of participation. The full strength of the school is the sum total of all its parts, with the age, abilities, experience, interests and ambitions of many groups of children and their teachers as variable factors. Seldom do we have the opportunity to see the energies and skills of everyone working concurrently; far too often isolated groups have the limelight, and for too many there is little enough chance to entertain and instruct their fellows. Schools make for themselves reputations, good and bad. Some do this through examination successes, others excel on the sports field or in music or drama. In practically all of these events far too many people appear only as passive spectators. My main thesis is that everyone has something to contribute, and by being encouraged to do so, during some festive occasion, they will feel a greater sense of belonging to an organisation. In terms of the building up of an *esprit de corps* (if that is not too archaic a term) such events are valuable.

Those teachers in the primary and secondary fields who are committed to the thematic approach to learning, are only too well aware of the pressures of time on the study that they and the class are committed to. In such situations, individual and group work flourishes, and at the end of the project the pieces are gathered together and presented so that everyone learns what the group as a whole has discovered. Similarly in celebrations and festivals, with so many children involved, a larger study and treatment can be attempted, knowing that all will see and hear what each section of the community has achieved.

Such occasions become highlights in the child's memories and perhaps provide some truth to the saying that these are the happiest days of their lives. I am always delighted when the children who are about to leave the school collaborate in a service of celebration and remind us (and themselves) of the festivals in which they have taken part. Often with singular ease they refreshed our memories by providing a song, some movement work or drama from the particular event in which they have participated. This kind of nostalgic journey into the past may not be typically childlike, but it reinforces the feeling of co-operative unity and almost timeless continuity which I think is basically tribal and worth preserving.

There are many ways of making a contribution to the success of a venture such as mentioned. Singing, drama and movement work are perhaps the most obvious manifestations. But creative writing, music, choral speaking, art and craft and various forms of audio-visual aids can all be used to great dramatic effect. The very essence of any celebration will be the variety of ways in which the theme is interpreted. Contributions will vary in quality and quantity, but each will play a part in the event. A festival can be compared to a street in which one can see a variety of shops. There is the large supermarket, one or two examples of chain stores, several shops which sell the same commodity, an old established family business, perhaps a market stall or two. The particular combination of shops, and their juxtaposition, their particular facades, and the ways in which they dress their windows and in other ways attract attention, give a certain identity to the community. Similarly the vitality of any celebration will ultimately depend upon the different approach and contribution of each group of people participating.

I would like to describe some early attempts at promoting co-operative enterprise in school. The first occasion was the result of a sponsored art competition in which the theme was The Jungle. The speed and enthusiasm with which everyone adopted this spoke as much for the obvious need for some stimulus as the interest in the subject matter. From children aged five to eleven all kinds of animals and scenes were produced. Various media were employed and different sizes and colours of paper adopted. Three-dimensional forms were attempted by some using clay, Plasticine, paper and wire. My own class was given the task of preparing the background — forest trees, creepers, exotic flower forms and so on. A large room was arranged with all the spare furniture we could find, including jumping stands, old easels and so on. Skipping ropes, with creeper wrappings, were strung from all the highest points, including the rafters. Then the pictures were pinned or pegged all over. The result was a glorious profusion of colour and shape which was quite an adventure to walk through. The two best efforts (a most difficult task to decide upon) were sent up and the children were duly presented with their book prizes but it was the memory of this first art celebration which remained for those children years afterwards.

The natural scene has always interested me and teaching as I was then in an old three-decker Victorian building surrounded by tenement blocks and factories, it was important for our children to feel some sense of the passing of the seasons. So as each new season came along during one year, a room was set aside and each class was invited to make some contribution towards the picture of autumn, or whatever. Pictures were painted using the natural specimens as a stimulus, collections were made in the local parks with the co-operation of the keepers, and models were made. For instance, there was a model showing all the forms of winter sports, when that season was being celebrated. One group made examples of nesting boxes and feeding tables, to start off others in this work.

Each class came up in turn, and looked around the exhibition, made drawings, and in some cases, answered questions on a quiz sheet that had been prepared for each age group. From each of the exhibitions, we collected some significant items which were not of a perishable nature, and at the end of the school year, a fifth display was mounted which reminded everyone of the continuing cycle of events. For this celebration, creative writing about features of each season which had seemed significant to the children was encouraged and examples in their best writing were carefully mounted among the leaves and branches.

The next excursion into a co-operative venture was still more ambitious. With my headmaster's approval I approached my colleagues to gain their interest in the Commonwealth. For a period of six weeks I asked each one to adopt one of the member countries and made a study of it with their classes. Perhaps the very idea and ideals of the Commonwealth enthused the staff and they quickly decided upon their choice. Two were interesting adoptions – India by a teacher lately from that country, and Malta, by a young member of staff with a boy friend from that island. As well as arranging for a loan of relevant books from the authority library and appropriate films – approximately two per class – I visited the Stationery Office and the Commonwealth Institute and bought a large supply of literature and booklets to provide further background knowledge and inspiration on each of the countries being studied. At the end of the school project, material was brought together in a hall display, which included pictures, models, examples of food, craft ware, and costumes worn by the children. Not only did the children enjoy this visit to 'foreign lands', they were also able to show their parents what they and their friends had found out together.

In 1961 I was given my own school and I decided that I wanted to develop this idea of the festival occasion further. The new staff were keen and opening a new school gave them pioneering zeal and energy. Drama had been a feature of two of my new colleagues' training, and musical talent was present in quality if not in quantity, and so the idea of celebration broadened out to take various expressive forms.

The work of the next few years, in which we had a festival every term (and even on occasions twice when the engines were at full throttle) I have described in my earlier book *A Book of Festivals*. What was learned from some twenty or so occasions, I would like to distil and detail in the next chapter. The particular feature of the first group of celebrations was the aim to concentrate all the effort into one afternoon. In the case of the Festival of Mathematics the sheer quantity of material forced us into having a second session during the following week, but by and large, we always hoped to produce a single neat picture illustrating the theme.

Since then the process of celebrating at Boxgrove has continued to evolve. Infants have now been combined with the Juniors, and so a large body of people – at times 500 in number – have come together to celebrate. Sometimes a Festival, e.g. Easter and even more in the case of Christmas – has spread over a longer period – even for as much as a fortnight. Films have been shown in preceding weeks to inform and stimulate the children. Displays of books and pictures are made with the same intention. Assemblies may act as a vehicle to illustrate some aspect of the theme from which some moral can be drawn.

What emerges is that there is no real formula for success except that enthusiasm, daring and some ability to communicate zest, are vital. For the rest, it seems that a profusion of events can be joined together and be presented in such a way that while being individualistic and enterprising, they do take on, promote and develop elements which make up the selected theme. From all of this a sense of artistic excitement, occasion and fun emerges – for everyone, we hope, and not just the organisers.

flying were making daring excursions off the ground. It was the beginning of the jazz age. On the other side of the coin, there was plenty of social unrest. The suffragettes were increasing their efforts for equal rights. There were strikes, lockouts and rioting such as seen in the Sidney Street siege. Certainly a remarkable year for examination.

SELLING THE IDEA

I am a firm believer in personal confrontation, and so when the time comes to introduce the theme, a number of the staff are approached because they are senior colleagues, have special interests such as music and drama, or a particular knowledge of the subject matter. It is a measure of the director's skill if he can interest others in an idea, and if he has already given time and thought to the matter, he will be able to suggest features of the scheme which are particularly attractive. Depending on the ability of the hearer to assimilate new suggestions, and their fertility of imagination, so the reaction will vary. Some people need days and even weeks to respond actively to an idea, while others are ready with immediate suggestions to add to the book. Usually the term before the event is soon enough for the gestation period of a project to begin; much longer and the whole event may be still-born.

At this early stage, others will hear on the grape-vine of the venture and so when approached themselves will not have the stunned and stony look that might have been the case without some prior knowledge. About four or five weeks before Celebration Day the scheme can be formally announced at the staff meeting, and everyone asked to contribute ideas and offers of particular help. Anxious new colleagues will approach the old hands for ideas and will be advised to wait for a week, and if they have not come up with anything original, then the director will make a few suggestions — he hopes appropriate to the age and past experience of the class and the ability of the teacher to cope with the particular activity. Often the close collaboration of a new teacher with an experienced teacher in the production of a short scene is suggested to both parties where there appears to be some lack of confidence. Where a teacher and his or her class have been invited to take an assembly during the week of the festival, they might well be excused performing in the main event, but they could be persuaded to link their religious worship with the theme. Children from that class may well be members of the choir, or instrumentalists, or have contributed a painting or a model. Where there has been a large offering of items, the director may well feel relieved not to have to lengthen the proceedings beyond a reasonable limit and so risk exhaustion.

Most teachers working in this kind of environment where festivals and other such occasions are part of the normal scheme of things, will want their classes to take part, but sometimes one has a less co-operative member of staff for whom none of the above overtures have worked. A number of courses are open to deal with this situation. A definite request can be made for the class to produce a particular item, which you know is well within the capacity of class and teacher. This should be prefaced with the request 'Do you think I could ask you to . . . ?' I prefer never to demand as a right, that which I can ask as a favour. I would leave a certain amount of interpretation to this teacher, rather than produce a blueprint which is likely to be followed very half-heartedly. The other alternative is to request some of the children to work on some smaller aspect of the theme with you, so that the class do not feel they have been left out.

The children will be introduced to the idea by their teachers, so that discussion and activity can proceed. Where a certain feature, e.g. a chorus for a song, is being learnt by the whole school, then a reminder is given – in a different way each time – of the forthcoming event (probably about three weeks ahead). With recent festivals, I have begun to prepare the ground early, by playing before and after assembly, music appropriate to the theme, e.g. Vivaldi's *Four Seasons* for our Festival of Autumn, Winter, Spring and Summer. To further prepare everyone's mind, stories and illustrations for assembly have been linked closely with the celebration theme, so that the particular event comes as a climax to as much as half a term's work, e.g. in the weeks preceding our Festival of Westminster Abbey, the children heard the story of St. Peter serving as a ferryman, Edward the Confessor, the fight between the soldiers and the escaped prisoners from the Tower who had sought sanctuary, the testing of the Pyx, the details of a Coronation and so on.

PUBLICITY

In addition to verbal persuasion, it is important to attract attention in other ways. An item in the school news sheet or termly magazine is a beginning. Posters can be prepared – a competition sponsored to discover the best one will pay dividends. A corridor, foyer, hall or library display of pictures, books and models before the celebration will get everyone in the mood, where some care has been taken not only in the selection of items, but the way in which they are displayed. The careful trimming and mounting of children's pictures is surely the least that they can expect. Where materials, flowers and other embellishments can be afforded, borrowed or . . . then they should be used to show everything else up with the greatest effect.

A programme, carefully designed (again a competition possibility) should feature the name of the celebration, its time and place, with a list of the various items to be presented. A brief note may be needed giving credits where necessary, and the synopsis of a story or song where the telling of it may not be abundantly clear. Issued in advance, programmes make good messengers of propaganda too. Where the local press are interested in school activities a mention of the forthcoming event can be featured.

PREPARATION
In the early stages, i.e. four weeks before the Festival, no extra time should be required by anyone unless the class and the teacher may be producing or helping to create more than one item. But in the last fortnight, it is hoped that the timetable, especially of the hall, is so flexible that those in need of extra time can ask for it. This will also mean that the head and others may be able to make their contributions by taking classes or groups of children while rehearsals are going on. Since the whole programme is intended for private consumption (but can and should include guests) then it is very important to strive for naturalness. Over-rehearsal is unlikely to achieve that spontaneity which is desirable. Audibility is vital, of course, and so is tuneful singing – although one does not expect the same standard as that produced by cathedral choristers. What we want is the sheer joy of singing coming over. To provide a balanced programme, it is to be hoped that drama and movement work will be featured. Most of my experience of these occasions has been in halls without a proscenium arch and curtains, and I would like to suggest that the event will seem less like a concert, and more like the celebrations suggested here, if the performance area is not separated from the audience. By the use of an arena rather than an apron stage the magic is not abandoned and the spell worked by performers can still be achieved in the midst of their friends.

Room to perform is required, of course, and during rehearsal a kind of euphoria sets in with all the great space of the hall to work in. So the final practice must be performed within the confines of the allotted area. A decision needs to be made on the requirements of each group. Where one or more would like to use a wall (particularly in our case the P.E. apparatus on one wall) then a horseshoe pattern is agreed upon. For the

Tongan Festival we sat in such a way that we left an oval space in the middle of the hall – as is the custom for celebrations on that Pacific island. For the St. Valentine occasion we left the shape of a heart in the middle of the hall. Both shapes were preserved by sticking strips of masking tape to the floor. This material is useful where other guide lines are needed, i.e. for entrances, and positions of drama blocks for various parts of the Celebrations. So that the actions can be seen, these flexible blocks can be used to raise people up to different levels and, at the same time, suggest palaces, space ships and whatever.

Where a school does a lot of drama work, a wardrobe may well have a large stock of clothes which have universal application, but it is worthwhile going to the expense of providing some new material for principal performers. An early decision needs to be made on what form these shall take – what head-dresses, masks, and other props are required, so that they can be made in good time. Where music is being used for movement work, then arrangements should be made to tape-record it. The same applies to any other sound or visual effects that are required.

FINAL PROGRAMMING

The director will have seen parts, if not the whole, of the various items being performed, and have a good idea of the running time. This will often be much shorter on actual performance – although the time apparently saved usually goes in the intervals between items. It is now an important part of the director's job to arrange the programme in such a way that there is a fluidity about the whole proceedings. This can be achieved by seating groups of people in places convenient for their starting positions – the choir arranged near the piano, and so on.

An interesting starter is needed for the celebration – and also for the second half, if an interval is required. The last item needs to be a good one (as does the one before the interval) – and that can quite appropriately be a rousing song, in which there could be audience participation. Twice we have chosen themes which very successfully cleared the hall, with the children going out in groups, at the commencement of various verses. These were to *Kum BaYah* (in a Celebration of Harvest) and to *Children Go Where I Send You* (during a Christmas programme).

The programme can be arranged where it does not affect any chronological plan, so that the first half requires a very limited number of drama blocks and more props, and the situation reversed in part two of the programme. It is a good idea for the director to be given a plan of the layout of the arena for each item, with a special note of any special effects, like use of microphone, tape recorder, slide projector, gramophone, lights, etc. and the name of children who are to operate, so that at the changeover between items he is ready to provide whatever extra assistance is required.

It is a good idea to arrange the programme so that the pace is varied, and put together items which are complementary — thus the song by one group may well bear directly on the same aspect of the music played by another section. Make sure that staff have seen a draft of the programme — items have been known to have been missed out — and other minds (although not too many) are valuable in suggesting more suitable arrangements. Duplicated sheets should be circulated as soon as possible when the details have been finalised. The children should also know at which point in the programme they will be making their contribution, but I prefer not to tell them too much about what others are doing, hoping that their enjoyment will be all the greater for this secrecy. I do like to remind them of the importance of the occasion, and the need for the full co-operation in making it a time of pleasure for all.

THE CELEBRATION

The hall will have been got ready beforehand. Pictures, backcloths and props for the first item can be placed ready. Drama blocks will be in position either in the arena or in corridors or adjacent rooms ready to be carried out. Tape recorders will be set up, switched on, and checked for track, speed, volume and starting position. Any other electric equipment needs to be checked, with extension leads if there are not enough sockets in the hall. Seating will be ready for parents and official guests, and they will have been reminded that the Celebration will start promptly.

The youngest children should come in first and take up their positions, joined soon afterwards by the older children. Appropriate music should be played to set the mood. A special signal of attention should be introduced, e.g. a ship's bell for the Celebration of Captain Cook's Voyages; a time pattern on percussion instruments for the Time Festival; marching feet for the anniversary of a battle.

The director will need to have done his homework and so provide linking commentary between items, and use the playlet, the song, the demonstration to illustrate dramatically some aspect of the theme. Where possible a member of each group should make the particular announcement of the item, and should explain briefly what is being done – especially where any misunderstanding of the plot might arise.

Such children need to be chosen for the clarity with which they can speak, and providing they have waited for silence (following the celebration theme signal) then they will command attention.

Where the programme is a long one, and young children are involved, their particular items are better included near the beginning, and, in fact, prepared as a unit. Because of the length of time involved, it is usually a good plan to suggest that they only see the first half of the programme – which can be arranged to suit their particular interests. Where a more elaborate and longer item is in the second half and may well be the closing item because of its high standard, this play or whatever, can be performed again the following day for the infants. The non-return of the young children will leave more room for seating and for the performance, and such a situation might again dictate which items appear after the interval.

Staff need to be seated in strategic positions around the hall to keep an eye open for incipient boredom which might manifest itself in secret warfare, childish curiosity in the props carried by the performers next in the ring, or the gradual destruction of the cardigan of the girl in front who is engrossed, by a boy who isn't.

If the programme appears to be over-running seriously, then the director may need to arbitrarily decide to cut it short. He will already have suspected this situation developing early in the proceedings and so will need to decide what to postpone. Where a group – e.g. the choir – have sung a number of times, then some of their repertoire could be left over. But it might mean leaving out a single offering by one class. An apology will have to be made and some special mention made of their work when the performance of it is finally made. The important thing is to get off to a good start with the proceedings. I have only once been secretly pleased when a Festival (of Time) started late. This allowed me to mention the treasonable story that during the Ceremony of the Trooping of the Colour, the Queen always arrives on the parade ground on time. This is achieved by the stopping of the clock – when necessary.

So we were able to start our Festival in the same fashion – on time – by the playing of a tape recording of Big Ben striking two exactly.

At the end of the performance, some brief words are needed to summarise the afternoon's events, and thank everyone for their contributions and co-operation.

AFTER THE CELEBRATION

The children will have been seen off – care taken with props and costumes, because they will be needed again, even for a repeat performance, possibly in front of a camera, or another audience.

The teachers will have had their imagination, creative ability and energies stretched to the point of exhaustion and will need some refreshment. The events of the afternoon will probably be gone over. Some may feel a little private agony, if they consider that their children have left only a vague impression rather than bring everything into sharp focus. These may need cheering up a bit, but by and large it will be a happy group of people who will see the results of their co-operative labours coming to fruition. One is reminded of the story of the elephant and the mouse who crossed the bridge together, and the remark made by the small creature, 'Didn't we make it shake?' I am always impressed when I hear those 'heavyweights' on the staff commenting on the bridge-shaking which some of their newer colleagues had caused. Perhaps they remembered the story of the other mouse, who was able to release its larger friend, the lion, from the ensnaring net of the hunter – and mice do grow into lions and elephants, in time.

I think that the director needs to do the rounds during the following day to congratulate everyone for their work, including people who have helped with costumes, received visitors as well as those who have shouldered the main work of producing an item for the celebration. Often guests will send a letter to the school, commenting on the performance, and this usually flattering message is pleasant to read out to the children when they next assemble together.

It is valuable within a few days of a celebration to try to look critically at all of it, and note weak features, including the organisation, and see what improvements can be suggested for the next occasion.

It is useful to keep a record of the festival programme notes, photographs and tape recordings of certain items. This is not just for historical interest. Often certain elements of one occasion are quite appropriate to another celebration, and much researching is saved. One of the interesting features of my school is the close association of the play centre activities with the day school. On occasions items prepared by the play centre staff have been included in our celebrations. The instant Festival of Tonga benefited from the help given by the teacher who taught dancing out of school hours, when we were given so little time before the arrival of our visitor. But it is the record of the school's history which the play centre are working on, which is so fascinating. This is the Boxgrove Tapestry. Each panel of hessian is six feet long and on it appear the events of a particular year in fabric collage. Naturally the Festivals, which are the highlights of our calendar, are well featured.

The next section of this book is a Tapestry of Celebrations. It will be seen that there is no rigid scheme, but rather an inexhaustible number of possibilities. It is not meant to be a mere collection of recipes, which, if conscientiously followed, will produce the perfect festival. Like those occasions listed in my *Book of Festivals*, these events have all been celebrated at Boxgrove, but to make their appeal more universal and to encourage selection, adaption and improvement, the information and suggestions have been enlarged. I hope what will come through in reading about the different festivals, is the spirit of co-operation and creative energy which needs to be shown by everyone, if the occasion is going to have any significance. Without doubt a certain degree of boldness is required before launching out on a celebration, but aim high. To provide a memorable event, it is no good being moderate. Nothing succeeds like excess and in any case we might feel along with Lewis Morris 'How far high failure overleaps the bounds of low success'.

Time for a celebration

Just as it is important in deciding what project to carry out with a class to consider where the particular emphasis lies, so with festivals, the bias, if any, requires some scrutiny at the planning stage. At Boxgrove we had already featured mathematics in a Festival of that name and as part of The Singing Street. In choosing 'Time' as the central theme both science and mathematics could play an important part. I recall from my own school days taking part in a Conversazione (a word with an interesting sound and connotation to it). This featured science, with experiments being demonstrated all over the building. I determined that such a demonstration could form an integral part of the festival, and for a few weeks before the celebration, six children worked with me on various experiments to do with time.

Plate 1 *A tense moment in The Thirteen Clocks.* (*Pace Ltd*)

There is apparently a very simple aspect of this subject, but quite soon as one reads about it, time becomes both abstract and complex, and while one is tempted to limit one's activities to an elementary treatment, there are some most inviting situations to explore within such a festival. What was a tremendous help in the planning phase was a number of radio programmes on The Nature of Time by G. J. Whitbrow, reprinted in *The Listener* (January 1970), and a series of TV broadcasts by Professor G. Porter which were the Christmas lecture programmes from the Royal Institute. The Professor provided some scintillating entertainment and knowledge in the programmes which were entitled, *In The Beginning, Moving Through Time and Space, The Tick of the Atom, Big Time, Little Time, Faster, Faster* and *To The Ends of Time.*

If one is planning ahead, and this is essential to the success of a venture like a festival, then the mind and eye are alert for anything even remotely connected with the theme, and so good fortune will favour the prepared mind.

A number of the schedules for seating plans, hall arrangements, positions for audio-visual aids, etc., are given overleaf since they relate to this programme, but for each occasion it is advisable to prepare these, circulate them, and make sure that anyone involved has a copy.

For this programme we needed two mains tape recorders and one portable battery tape recorder, one 8 mm cine projector, one film slide projector and stand, three screens (already fixed in position), one record player, five drama blocks and one set of steps, in different places and in varying quantities during the afternoon. Four tapes had been prepared and three records were needed at various times. Careful organisation of these aids and the rehearsal of those children and teachers who are going to synchronise their use with the action is necessary. It can all be achieved without fuss, if the same degree of importance is attached to this as to any other feature of the festival programme. Although in all likelihood there will be no formal script, after the situation has been discussed and worked through a number of times, a simple cueing sheet can be prepared.

Fig 1 Four different seating plans.
a. Alice in Wonderland – *X marks the position for the various excerpts.*

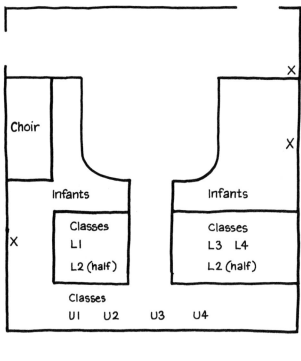

b. *Science Conversazione.*

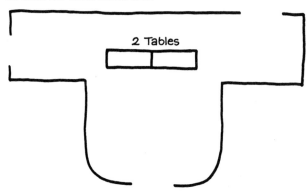

c. Apollo moon shot – the hall should be blacked out.

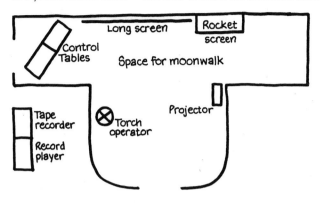

d. Four Seasons – ballet and poems (black out hall).

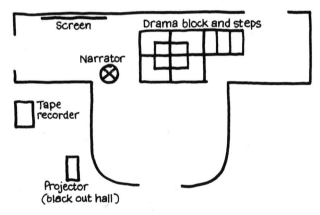

INFORMATION AND INSPIRATION
Books
Adler, Irving: *Time in Your Life* (Dobson).
Asimov, Isaac: *The Clock We Live On* (Abelard Schuman).
Carle, D: *British Time* (Crosby Lockwood).
Fleet, Simon: *Clocks* (Weidenfeld and Nicolson).
Gaidsmit, Sam and Claiborne, R: *Time* (Time Life International).
Goaman, Muriel: *Fun With Time* (Pelham Books).
Hood, Peter: *How Time Is Measured* (Oxford).
Herbert, A. P.: *Sundials Old and New* (Methuen).
Ilin, H.: *What Time Is It?* (Routledge and Kegan Paul).

Plate 2 Ready for blast-off.
(Pace Ltd)

Naylor, A. H.: *Study Book of Time and Clocks* (Bodley Head).
Priestley, J. B.: *Man and Time* (Aldous).
Purton, Rowland: *Man Tells The Time* (Hamish Hamilton).
Sullivan, N.: *Animal Timekeepers* (Phoenix).
Ward, F. A. B.: *Time Measurement* (HMSO).
Wright, Lawrence: *Clockwork Man* (Elek).
Ziner, F. and Thompson, Elizabeth: *True Book of Time* (Muller).
Time – a booklet report from the Schools Council Project at Bristol
University.

Poetry

There is obviously a vast number of poems which could be said to have
a link with time in its broadest sense. This is merely a short list which
will give pointers to other writing.
Barham, R. H.: *Ingoldsby Legend* (in which a husband is pursued by
his wife as a grandfather clock).
Auden, W. H.: *Sext, Nones, Vespers, Compline* and *Stop All the Clocks.*
Blunt, W. S.: *The Two Highwaymen* (Death and Time).
Browning, Robert: *Pippa's Song.*
Clare, John: *Clock-a-clay.*
Emmson, William: *Missing Dates.*
Hardy, Thomas: *The Clockwinder.*
Hood, T.: *Time of Roses.*
Hubbard, Robert: *Time.*
Johnson, J. W.: *The Creation.*
Keats, John: *To Autumn.*
Sendak, Maurice: *Chicken Soup With Rice* (Scholastic Book Services).
Shakespeare, W.: *When I do count the clock.*
Wain, John: *Time Was.*
Wordsworth, W.: *Written in March.*

There are also a number of nursery rhymes and simple poems which are
amongst the first to be learned at a mother's knee. Perhaps because
they all have this common denominator of time, its importance in our
daily lives is stressed.
Hickory Dickory Dock.
Cobbler Cobbler mend my shoe.
Solomon Grundy, born on Monday.
Polly put the kettle on.
Monday's child is fair of face.
Sneeze on Monday, sneeze for danger.

Wee Willie Winkie.
Thirty days hath September.

Music
Anderson, Leroy: *Syncopated Clock.*
Beethoven, L: *Allegro for a musical clock* (arranged by Fritz Spiegel).
Haydn, J: *The Clock Symphony* (3rd movement).
Kodaly, Z.: *Hary Janos Suite* (Viennese clock music).
Ponchielli: *The Dance of the Hours.*
Suppé: *Morning, Noon and Night.*
Dashing way with the smoothing iron.
Turn, turn, turn.
The grandfather clock.
The clock carol.
Three o'clock grandad – a kind of operetta by John Parry from
Music Workshop in BBC Schools programmes. (Pamphlets and
teachers' notes from BBC, 35 Marylebone High Street, London.) Peter
and Jill are asked to dispose of the family grandfather clock. With the
grumbling help of the carrier, Ebenezer, the clock passes from one
person to another, each living alternately at the top of the hill and the
bottom, until finally it finds a last resting place – back with Peter and Jill.

Excursions
Time Gallery of the Science Museum, London.
Royal Observatory, Greenwich.
Navigation Room, National Maritime Museum, Greenwich.
Planetarium, Baker Street, London, W.1.
Planetarium, Greenwich.
Small party visits to a watch menders and to a local church to see the
works of the clock.
Visits to airport or terminal railway or bus station to time arrivals and
departures.

CREATIVE ACTIVITIES
Written Work
Write in dialogue form the events of a rocket flight to and from the moon.

Write a story about the night you were locked inside a watchmaker's
shop. Reference to *The Pawn Shop* featuring Charlie Chaplin might
encourage a humorous approach.

Write a story about a device which can transport you into a different era. Decide upon the device and make this a group project to produce a book with the same central characters in each episode. Inspiration from BBC serial, *Dr. Who; Traveller in Time*, Alison Uttley; *The Gauntlet*, R. Welch; *The Ship That Flew*, H. Lewis; *Tom's Midnight Garden*, Phillipa Pearce; *The Story of the Amulet* and *Five Children and It*, E. Nesbit; *A Yankee at the Court of King Arthur*, Mark Twain; *The Long Christmas Dinner*, Thornton Wilder; *The Magic Mountain*, Thomas Mann.

Compose a short poem and set it to music using tuned percussion instruments – to use as a time or intermission signal.

Produce a piece of writing which includes as many of the following phrases as possible – save time, lose time, kill time, beat time, tell the time, ask the time, be behind time, take one's time, gain time, bide your time, serve your time, do time, half time, time after time, in good time, waste time, near her time, her time drawing near, etc.

Tempus Fugit is one of the conventional mottoes found on a sundial. Invent a suitable statement for today which is rendered in English.

Write a story in which other expressions about time are used, e.g. the year of the cattle sickness; the day of the great storm; the time of the leaf fall.

Write a letter to Smith's Clock and Watch Division for a booklet – *How They Work.*

Write to Westclox, Strathleven, Dumbarton, for a booklet *Stop The Clock*. (A letter of thanks is appreciated by all P.R. Departments.)

Drama and Movement

Act the story of Joshua and the day he stopped the sun (Joshua 10).

Act the Polynesian legend of How Maui caught the sun.

Use Holst's Planets' Suite and create the Universe, with the planets moving around their orbits in time.

Study Pieter Brueghel's picture *Triumph of Time*, and create a play or mime from it.

There are several references in *Alice* to time, reminding one of the mathematical background of the author. Create a number of very short sketches which could serve as linking sequences: Alice meets the March Mare; Meets the Duchess; Meets the Caterpillar; Meets the Mock Turtle; At the Trial of the Knave of Hearts; Meets Tweedledum and Tweedledee; Meets the Queens; Meets Humpty Dumpty; Becomes a Queen.

Write poems about the months or seasons; compose music to suit the mood of the seasons; costume children to fit the seasons and develop a movement sequence. Vivaldi's music *The Four Seasons*, and the BBC record, *The Seasons* (Music and words) will be helpful. Also the BBC record, *Sounds of the Countryside*, RED 60 M, used with a series of slides showing various aspects of the seasons, could provide interesting background to a ballet sequence. Slides owned by friends — showing places and faces — can be looked at with an eye for seasonal colour and pattern.

Make a journey into the past to interview Julius Caesar about the calendar, and the origin of the names of the months.

Similarly perform a pageant showing the Teutonic and Norse gods who gave their names to the days of the week.

Round the World in Eighty Days — Jules Verne — hangs on the day lost by crossing the International Date Line. Act part or the whole of the story.

Act the story of the Race to the Poles between Scott and Amundsen.

Organise a space machine to take a journey into the future and see what is in store for children in the year 2000. (Ray Bradbury's story *Fahrenheit 451* might stimulate some ideas.)

Perform the story of the Hare and the Tortoise as a puppet play.

Tell the story of King Canute to whom might be credited the proverb — Time and Tide Wait For No Man.

The Seven Ages of Man as described by Shakespeare in *As You Like It* Act II, Scene VII, can be used to stimulate scenes to show man at these various stages.

Produce a playlet about a Day at the Abbey, with the work and prayer of the monks carefully controlled by the bell and time.

Produce a *This Is Your Life* programme of a member of staff. (This can be done without the victim knowing – it happened to me much to my consternation because I thought I knew at least half that goes on in my own school.)

Read *The Thirteen Clocks* by James Thurber. Ask children to write poems about episodes in the story. Set these to music for choir and solo voices. Perform the operetta.

Science and Mathematical activities
Discover the use of the time bell on board ship and use this to 'order' a day at school, with watches taken by children.

Use a map and divide it into time zones, e.g. 12 noon in Britain, 7 a.m. in New York. If a number of clocks are available, set these to correspond to different times in the world.

Check the pulses of each child in the class, after quiet, and then vigorous activities (the latter repeated after five-minute intervals).

Make up a time chart to show personal histories and world history (illustrate this with historical and geographical pictures).

Acquire a cross-section of timber and count the annual rings. Place pins with small marked flags in the rings – which correspond to years since a particular event, counting from the outside edge.

Burn a candle and measure the height of unmelted wax at half-hourly intervals. Stick pins in a new candle at these intervals and use as a clock.

Prepare a pendulum and suspend it from a hook in a doorway. Measure the length of the string, swing the pendulum, and use a stopwatch to measure the time taken for ten complete swings. Alter length of pendulum, weight of pendulum bob and height of swing, timing the experiment carefully. Discover the variable and non-variable factors. Produce a graph showing length of pendulum with time of swing. What length of pendulum produces a one-second swing?

On a sunny day, erect a shadow stick and mark the length and direction of the shadow with chalk. Transfer information to a sheet of graph paper. Check at a later time in the year, after painting in each line and noticing its time. Make up a human sundial, using a child as the gnomon.

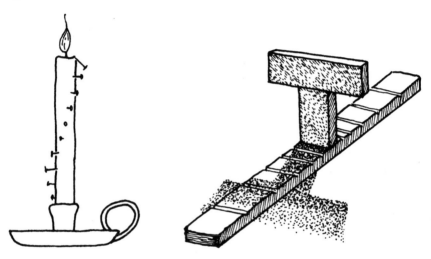

Fig 2 Candle clock.   *Fig 3 Egyptian shadow clock.*

Produce a series of statistics, e.g. the time taken for a child of each age group to run over a measured course in the playground; time taken by teachers to travel to school each day by various means of transport; time taken by children following different routes to walk home; the way temperature rises during the day; amount of time used by various children – sleeping, eating, at school, watching TV, playing, reading or other recreation; which month for birthdays.

Make up a series of graphs based on the above information and produce questions on them to make use of the information gathered (See various books from Nuffield Mathematics Project, published by Chambers and Murray, for further ideas.)

If an 8 mm camera is available, make a film which will show that certain actions are reversible and others are irreversible. For instance, bouncing a ball, riding on a swing, drinking from a cup (if level of liquid cannot be seen) can be shown backwards or forwards without causing comment but the tearing-up of paper, pouring liquid, knocking over a set of bricks, walking, sitting down and crossing legs become quite humorous when shown in reverse. Some more sophisticated cameras have different speeds and a sequence can be filmed at a fast speed and shown at a different rate. A further refinement would be the making of a time lapse sequence of a flower opening, or, just as spectacular, the movement of clouds when there is about 50 per cent cover. (Various Walt Disney nature pictures showed this technique to perfection.)

This opportunity should be grasped to teach children the order of days, months and seasons. A college lecturer visiting a student at the school was most impressed with the adopted topic of Time going on in class, but much saddened to find that the most elementary matter had not been covered — because so many of the children could not tell the time accurately! This would surely be the opportunity to use such books as Working With Time by R. H. Nichols and H. Howarth (Basil Blackwell) and Measuring Time by Tom H. Flanagan (Blackie). All of this, so that they can tell the time, estimate time, speeds, use a timetable, a 24-hour clock, etc.

For approximately £5, a clock kit can be purchased from Thwaites and Reed Ltd., 15 Bowling Green Lane, London, E.C.1. The parts can be assembled into a working clock, the movement of which can be observed through the plastic case.

Art
Draw a picture of an important athletic event. The playing of the relevant track of the BBC Radio Enterprises record, REC 29M (Highlights of Sports' Reports) which features the first 4-minute mile of Roger Bannister may act as an inspiration, or a reading of the crucial section in Roger Bannister's own book, The First Four Minutes (Putnam), or a showing of World Record Mile, a film on hire from Rank Library.

Make up a composite picture of a watchmakers' shop. Use this as a background for a collection of clocks and watches (it is surprising how many time pieces — in need of repair — will come in).

Make an illustration of Old Father Time greeting the New Year Baby.
Design a series of birthday cards for particular age groups – one year
old, five, eighteen, fifty, one hundred.

Make up a large group picture of a golden wedding celebration.

A pair of capsules, four feet in diameter, made of stainless steel, were
buried at Osaka, as part of Japan's Expo 70 celebration. Inside seven
objects were to be enclosed, as typical of the culture of the twentieth
century. They would be unearthed in 5,000 years' time. (It is interesting
to conjecture that 5,000 years ago, Abraham had not made his historic
journey from Ur of the Chaldees and the Pyramids had not yet been
built.) What objects (or models of these) would you place in the
capsule? Draw and colour your choice for posterity.

Craft

Drawing inspiration from Heath Robinson, invent a device to serve as
an alarm clock for a heavy sleeper.

Construct a number of time-marking devices, e.g. an Egyptian shadow
stick; a sand clock; a sinking bowl clock; a clepsydra; a pendulum;
a sun dial; a scratch dial on the wall; a ten-second timer, using a
sloping strip of wood with baffles, and a marble.

Make up a model of Stonehenge (see *What is Stonehenge?* H.M.S.O.
and the film *Stonehenge* – Gateway Films).

Design a calendar in cardboard and paper. Attempt to make this useful
for other years than this one. There are a number of commercial designs
to provide examples. There is a wooden calendar composed of a frame,
two cubes to cover all the number combinations and two sets of three
rectangular pieces – one for all the months, and the other for the seven
days of the week with a blank to preserve the symmetry of design.
The blocks are changed around as the date, day and months alter.

From broken clocks and watches make up a collage of dials, cogs,
hands, etc.

Inside a box, make up a model of Miss Havisham in her time-arrested
wedding-breakfast room.

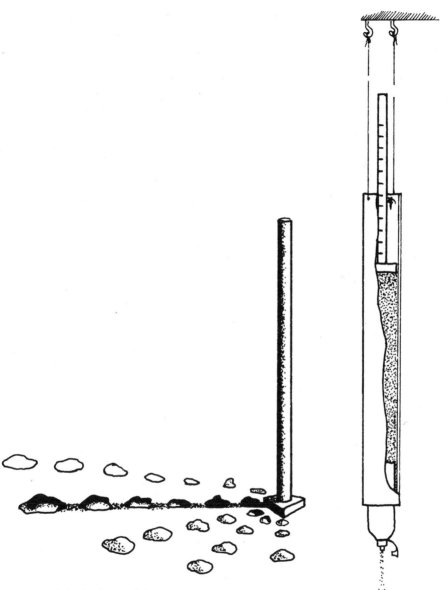

Fig 4 A shadow stick.

Fig 5 *A sand timer made from a cardboard tube into which a polythene soap bottle has been fixed. The sand flows through the hole at a steady rate and this is noted by the calibrated plunger rod which is placed on top of the sand.*

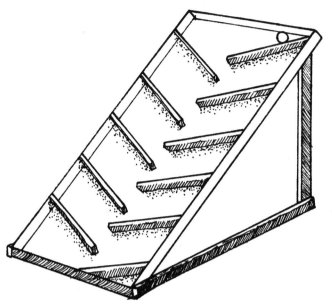

Fig 6 A 10-second marble timer. The time taken for the marble to go from top to bottom will be constant and so this device can be used as a timer.

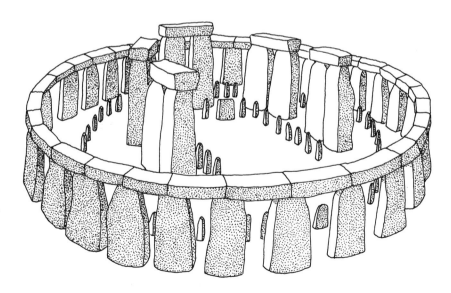

Fig 7 Clay block model of Stonehenge.

Make up a set of puppets of Peter Pan and his friends – and perform the story by J. M. Barrie.

Links with other festivals
The Molecule Club which is responsible for occasional productions at the Mermaid Theatre, Puddle Dock, London E.C.4, have pioneered a number of interesting productions in which demonstrations are mingled with song, dance and music-hall comedy. Their science-through-theatre productions have been *Lights Up*, *O.K. for Sound* and *Help* (devoted to the principles of mechanics).

The Forty-Five

Everyone loves a hero – especially a romantic figure – trying to overcome impossible odds. Such a one was Charles Edward Stuart. The ballad writers of the time took him to their hearts and wrote songs of his exploits – perhaps forgetting too easily the misery and cruelty which followed him in Scotland's history. The subject is well documented and as such is a good one for celebration. We chose to make this an activity which featured a very large choir – some hundred-strong. Eight songs were chosen and arranged to tell the story chronologically. The selection of suitable material depended upon the way in which the story line was carried along: tunefulness and a chorus in which the audience could be invited to join.

The songs were duplicated, put in an illustrated cover and stapled together with a strip of Royal Stuart tartan (which material the majority of the girls managed to wear for the event). Scottish country dancing was introduced twice – at moments of joyful celebration – the August 19 gathering at Glenfinnan and the arrival in Edinburgh later that month.

The newest development for this celebration was the use throughout the programme of projected slides and the spotlighting of other features, route maps, the Stuart Standard, etc. Tape-recorded sounds of marching feet, pipes, pistol and cannon fire and other kinds of battle were used. It was necessary therefore to produce a careful story board for this type of programme. Here is a section to indicate one form of procedure.

Script	Song	Dance	Slide	Sound
. . . new recruits joined from the villages and glens as they marched along.	Uist Tramping Song		Flag	
The Highlanders captured Perth and went on to Edinburgh which they took without a fight . . . . although the Castle held out. The Prince and his followers were happy and confident.		Petronella	Edinburgh Castle	

Script	Song	Dance	Slide	Sound
The English army under Sir John Cope had retreated in fright before this growing army of Highlanders.	Hey Johnnie Cope			
Johnny Cope and his army were soundly defeated in ten minutes at the Battle of Prestonpans.			Prestonpans battlefield	Gunfire
Now the Prince turned his army towards England and they soon crossed the border – a great army fresh from victory, led by the pipers.	Wi' a Hundred Pipers		Pipers	Pipe music
In England and Wales there were a large number of Jacobites who drank a toast to 'The King Across the Water' in glasses engraved with the white rose. But they might have been willing to raise their glasses but not their swords because very few joined Charles on his way South . . .			Stuart engraved glasses	

We received a message from the 1745 Association which ran as follows:

> This Association's chief aim is to keep green the memory of the brave men and women who suffered in the '45. In song and dance your pupils will be acting out a story of great courage and sadness. The Highlanders who fought in the '45 Rising were led by chiefs who realised from the first that they were staking everything in a losing cause. It is because they knew that, yet sacrificed everything

that they had to give for their honour and for what they believed to be right, that we in Scotland will always be proud of them, and will never allow their names to perish.

In these modern times, when nations and peoples are trying harder than ever before to understand one another, it is good to learn that the pupils of a London school will be re-telling the story of Prince Charlie. To his Highland followers this young prince did not stand for the claims of a Royal House alone. They saw him also as their leader in a cause which they, like their forefathers, were pledged to defend – the freedom of an ancient people, and everything they understood as their own way of life. If Culloden was a military defeat, it was no less a victory for the free spirit of man. And this is something which – whether in terms of history or the world today – all people of goodwill should unite to salute.

We send you our greetings, and our very good wishes for 26th November.

Marion Campbell. Hon. Secretary.

We were able to invite a piper, a lady, to play for us at the beginning of the Celebration and accompany the choir and audience when they sang the final song *Will Ye No Come Back Again?* I would think that any large city in the British Isles shelters at least one piper, and the presence of one in full regalia is a fine sight, and sound.

SOURCES OF INSPIRATION
Information books
Prince Charles Edward and the '45, Winifred Duke (Hale).
In the Steps of Bonnie Prince Charlie, Winifred Duke (Rich).
Argyll in the '45, Sir James Ferguson (Faber).
Bonnie Prince Charlie, Sylvia Haymon (Macdonald).
The Prince in the Heather, Eric Linklater (Hodder and Stoughton).
Ships of the '45, John S. Gibson (Hutchinson).
The Quest Forlorn, C. H. Hartmann (Heinemann).
The Young Adventurer, D. Nicholas (Batchworth).
The Life and Adventures of Prince Charles Edward Stuart, W. B. Norrie.
The Jacobite Movement, Sir Charles Petrie (Eyre and Spottiswoode).
Culloden, John Prebble (Penguin).
The Highland Clearances, John Prebble (Penguin).

The Jacobite Rising of 1745, William Stevenson (Longman).
Glenfinnan and the '45, I. C. Taylor and Jean Munro (Nat. Trust for
    Scotland).
Culloden, Col. Cameron Taylor (Nat. Trust for Scotland).
The Jacobite General, K. Tomasson (Blackwood).
Battle of the '45, K. Tomasson and F. Buist.
Flora Macdonald, Elizabeth Gray Vincey (Bles).

Stories
Midwinter, John Buchan (Nelson).
The Flight of the Heron ⎤
The Gleam in the North ⎬ D. K. Borster (Heinemann).
The Dark Mile ⎦
Lantern over the Lunes, Kathleen Fidler (Lutterworth).
The Hunted Head, Olivia Fitzroy (Cape).
The Escape of the Prince, Jane Lane (Evans).
The Young Inverey, John Niven (Faber)
The Heir of Craigs, Charles Vipont (Oxford).

Poetry
Lament for Culloden, R. Burns.
A Jacobite Toast, John Byrom.
A Jacobite's Epitaph, Lord Macauley.
Poems and Ballads of Scottish History, edited by Dewar M. Robb
    (Blackie).

Songs
To evoke a sense of place and time.
Eriskay Love Lilt.
Uist Tramping Song
Johnnie Cope
Wi' a Hundred Pipers.
Charlie is my Darling.
Come o'er the stream, Charlie.
Skye boat song.
Will ye no come back again?
Scotland the brave.

Words and music for these better known songs can be found in a
variety of song books. These and many more can be found in
Prince Charlie and the '45, arranged by Alan Reid (Bayley and Ferguson).

46

See also Topic Record 12T79, *The Jacobite Rebellions,* and
Leader Record, LER 3002, *The Fate o' Charlie.*

There are many records on the catalogues which include at least one
of the better known songs, e.g. Decca's *The World of Scotland,* SPA41.
There are also books such as *Songs of Scotland,* Books 1 and 2,
edited by Granville Bentock (Paxton), where this celebration is only
one part of a larger study of Scotland.

Dances
Reels, Strathspeys and Country Dances, arr. John Longmire (Paxton).
EMI have a large selection of recorded Scottish music, e.g. Eightsome
Reel, Gay Gordons and Bluebell Polka, GEP8937; Dashing White
Sergeant, Highland Laddie Reel, Duchess of Atholl's Slipper, etc.,
PVS 7018.

The Royal Scottish Country Dance Society issues six 45rpm records,
e.g. The Reel — The Sandal and Jig — Two by Two, EDP001;
Strathspey — New Park and Jig — The Rakish Highlander, EPD002.

Other music
Four Scottish Dances, Malcolm Arnold.
Scottish Suite, Iain Hamilton.
Scotch Symphony, Felix Mendelssohn.
Judas Maccabeus, G. F. Handel (written to celebrate the victory of
    Culloden).

Films
Tartans of Scotland (Scottish Film Library).
Wild Highlands (British Transport Films Ltd.).

Excursions
Museums: West Highland Museum, Fort William.
          Glencoe Museum.

Sites: Glenfinnan.
          Culloden.

Other aids
Jackdaw Archives Material: *The '15 and the '45* (Cape).
The Raising of the Standard (map folder — National Trust for Scotland).

Bonnie Prince Charlie Map (Bartholomew).
Jacobite Rising (filmstrip — Hulton Press).

Useful addresses
The National Trust for Scotland
5 Charlotte Square
Edinburgh 2

Scottish Tourist Board
2 Rutland Place
Edinburgh 1

Highlands and Islands Development Board
P.O. Box 7, Inverness

The 1745 Association
Invercoe House
Glencoe, Argyll

Braemar Films Ltd. (for catalogue of slides)
P.O. Box 1, Newton Mearns, Glasgow

Hamilton Tait Ltd. (for catalogue of slides)
141 Bruntisfield Place
Edinburgh

Walton Sound and Film Services
87 Richford Street,
London, W.6.

Atkinson, Baldwin & Co. Ltd.
44 Glass House Street, London, W.1
(Coloured photograph of Bonnie Prince Charlie and leaflet about
    Drambuie liqueur.)

CREATIVE ACTIVITIES
Written work
The news of the Prince's landing reaches your glen. Your mother does
not want you to go, but you later follow your father to the lochside
where you see Charles Edward Stuart for the first time. Write about
this day.

48

Write a poem about the first march eastwards towards Edinburgh as the army grows. Make the last line of each verse a rallying call. Tape record your poem and add the sound of kettledrums and marching feet. The Battle of Culloden is over. You manage to escape with the Prince. Tell your story of the first hours after the defeat.

Prepare a 'wanted' notice for the Prince.

Write a newspaper report on the departure of the Prince.

Drama and movement work
Select a number of incidents from the story of the Rebellion and make a series of dramatic scenes to be linked by a narrator. E.g. the conversation between Charles and the reluctant Cameron; the argument at Derby when the rebels returned to Scotland; the Flora Macdonald episode.

Select songs from the saga, e.g. *Hey Johnnie Cope* and produce a mime to go along with the story.

After Culloden Prince Charles revealed his courage and cheerfulness on many occasions. Act a scene in which he helps to cook a meal over a camp fire and then joins in the revelry of singing and dancing.

Art
Prepare pictures showing the arrival of the Prince on the Isle of Eriskay on July 23rd, 1745, from a French ship.

Make a map of the British Isles showing the route taken by Prince Charles.

Draw a portrait of Prince Charles Edward Stuart.
Prepare a picture, using crayon, of a highland pipe band.
(Play a record of bagpipe music during the production of the picture – and after its completion.)

Craft
Make up a model of the battle of Culloden. Simple paper cut-out figures, after decoration to be fixed into a diorama scene (see 1066).

Make a tape-recorded loop of battle noises – simulated or dubbed from a sound effects record.

Fig 8 Simple model made up inside a box — Flora Macdonald helps Bonnie Prince Charlie to escape.

Make a model of Flora Macdonald and the Prince escaping in a rowing boat.

Prepare a collection of figures of men dressed in the correct tartan of those clans which took part in the events of 1745 and 1746. (See *Clans and Tartans of Scotland* — Robert Bain.)

Using a large wooden armature or a tailor's dummy, dress a highlander. Prepare a memorial stone in paper of all those clans which fought at Culloden. Use candle to apply letter of Clan Macdonald, etc., and then apply paint which will be resisted over the wax areas.

Links with other celebrations
Hereward the Great against William the Conqueror, 1069.
Lady Jane Grey against Mary Tudor, 1553.
Thomas Wyatt, the poet, against Mary Tudor 1554.
Mary Queen of Scots against Elizabeth in the Rebellion of the North.
Ridolphi Plot.
Throckmorton Plot.
Babington Plot, 1560–1585.
Princess Elizabeth against Jame 1, 1605.
Duke of Monmouth against James II, 1685.

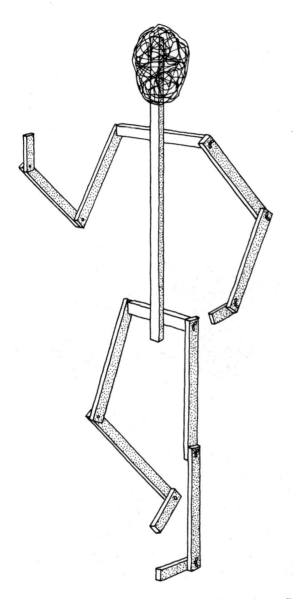

Fig 9 Wooden armature for modelling a large figure.

The Norman Invasion

'They're coming!' I can recall those words vividly — although I said them thirty-five years ago — because with them I opened a pageant (to raise money for a set of new school gates). As I rushed onto the arena shouting this warning, just ahead of William the Conqueror riding on a fine white horse, I little realised that this pageant from history would remain with me as one of the few significant memories of my secondary school days (see the Time Festival for another). Perhaps five years before this, I recall being taken a hundred miles to see a great historical pageant at York. The floodlit spectacle kept a six-year-old wide awake well after his normal bed-time and perhaps then were sown the seeds of ambition to plan and organise such celebrations!

It was just at the turn of the century (which was before my time!) that a great pageant was staged at Sherborne in the castle grounds, and such was its success, that a fashion for that kind of event resulted. Louis Parker (who significantly was also christened Napoleon) was the Pageant Master on that and some subsequent occasions. The historians might like to know that Sherborne was staged 1905, Warwick 1906, Bury St. Edmunds 1907, Dover 1908, and Colchester and York in 1909 — in other words at least a year was required for preparation of productions on this scale.

Frank Lascelles was one of those in the audience at Warwick and his imagination was sufficiently fired for him to produce a pageant himself at Oxford. This began a long career as Pageant Master all over the world and at least two significant titles were conferred upon him. One by the Basuto tribesmen who took part in the South African celebrations in Capetown was "Rakalello" which means "Father of Beautiful Thoughts". The other was conferred on him by the Iroquois Indians who also took part happily with the the white people in the Quebec Pageant of 1908. They called him "Tehonikonraka" or "A Man Full of Resource". One can always hope that every pageant master has these qualities in some degree. Perhaps Lascelles's greatest production was the Pageant of Empire in 1924, when 15,000 Londoners assembled at Wembley to celebrate.

The ladies have also been represented in this work and one of the greatest was Gwen Lilley who could claim Tewkesbury 1931 and Runnymede 1934 amongst her battle honours. Most recently David Clarke can be included because of his production of the great Pageant on England held in Guildford in 1968.

It is interesting to note the advent of another art form – *Son et Lumière* – in which the disembodied voices of distinguished actors and actresses relate the history of some particular great building, with rooms and areas lit in some special way to focus attention on them. Such sophisticated treatment of a historical situation is very compelling to watch and does allow the imagination of the audience to interpret the scene. However, it can be argued that the spontaneity is somewhat lost when those taking part in the performance are merely voices.

In 1968 a group of friends with an interest in military affairs met in Oxford to discuss the tactical pattern of the Civil War. The suggestion that armies were raised to re-enact the battle was adopted and within eight months they had re-fought the Battle of Edgehill. The 200 who took part in that affray grew to 700 when, a year later, there was a re-run of the Battle of Marston Moor. The organisation has now been invited to partake in other such celebrations and details can be got from the Adjutant-General of the Sealed Knot, Hastings Road, Orchard Corner, Firgrove Hill, Farnham, Surrey.

Now back to more modest affairs. Following book research and references to the multitude of colour supplements, feature articles in teaching journals, and viewing of projected materials, the children visited Hastings, Pevensey and Battle. The culmination of their work was to be a Pageant of 1066. A loudspeaker system to provide amplified commentary, conversation (pre-recorded in some cases) and music was hired from the local Borough Council for £2 – for one day. Signposts were prepared with bold labels so that the audience knew where Stamford Bridge, London, Bosham, Senlac Hill, etc. were. Coat trolleys were pressed into service as Norman ships; weapons, armour and costumes were manufactured, and the children rehearsed in their story. This particular event has much to commend it with plenty of incident and some good opportunities for characters to be filled out. Even more, it has the great advantage of requiring an almost unlimited number of participants!

INFORMATION AND INSPIRATION
Books

Barclay, Brigadier C. N: *Battle 1066* (Dent).
Denny, N. and Filmer-Sankey, J: *The Bayeux Tapestry* (Collins).
Douglas, David: *William the Conqueror.*

Duggan, Alfred: *Growing up in the Norman Conquest* (Faber).
Furneaux, Rupert: *Conquest 1066* (Warburg).
Latham, R. E: *Finding out about the Normans* (Muller).
Lemmon, Lt. Col. C. H: *The Field of Hastings* (Allan).
Peach, L. du Garde: *William the Conqueror* (Wills and Hepworth).
Sellman, R. W: *Norman England* (Methuen).
Sturton, Sir Frank and others: *The Bayeux Tapestry* (Phaidon).
Unstead, R: *Mediaeval Scene* (Black).

Historical fiction
Baker, George: *Hawk of Normandy* (Lutterworth).
Bryher, A: *Fourteenth of October* (Collins).
Heyer, Georgette: *The Conqueror* (Heinemann).
Muntz, Hope: *The Golden Warrior* (Chatto and Windus).
Treece, Henry: *Hounds of the King* (Bodley Head).

Films
The Bayeux Tapesty (from EFVA).
Mediaeval Monastery
Mediaeval Village   (from Rank Films).
Mediaeval Castle

Filmstrips
The Norman Conquest (Visual Information Services).
High the Norman Page (Hulton).
The Bayeux Tapestry (Rank).
William the Conqueror (Wills and Hepworth — to be used in conjunction with their Ladybird book of the same name).
William I (Rank).

Other aids
A 'newspaper' for October 25th, 1066 — *Hastings Observer* (from Information bureau at Hastings).

Pictures in Macmillan's History Series 1 *Norman Warriors*
Norman Ships
Norman Castle
English Village, Early Norman
Hunting Party.

Excursions

Pevensey, Sussex — site of landing.

Battle Abbey, Sussex — for guided tour.

Hastings — castle and Triodome to see model of battlefield and Hastings, and embroidery, two panels of which illustrate the Invasion.

Westminster Abbey.

Colchester.

Chepstow.

Such a study as this, resulting in a pageant or other form of celebration, would inevitably lead to an extension of the study. Thus the children would want to know what were the results of the Norman invasion. In this enlarged framework visits could be made to Norman castle and churches built at the end of the 12th century. For instance, the Tower of London, Rochester, Richmond (Yorks), Castle Hedingham (Essex), Dover, etc.

Norman church architecture can be seen in St. John's Chapel, Tower of London; Portchester (Hampshire); Peterborough Cathedral; Selby Abbey (Yorks); Birkin (Yorks); Tewkesbury; Gloucester; Glastonbury; Fountains Abbey, etc.

About 600 churches were built in all and particularly recommended are the following which have survived with only minor repairs and alterations: St. Nicholas, Barfreston, Kent.

St. Michael's and All Angels, Stewkley, Bucks.

St. John's Adel, Yorks.

If on a school journey to that part of France, a visit ought to be made to the public library at Bayeux to see the 230-foot long tapestry — which, like the date 1066, seems to be one of the few items of common general knowledge held by every child.

A very good alternative is to visit Reading Museum and Art Gallery and see a facsimile which was created in the 1880s by thirty-five ladies of Leek in Staffordshire. Eight different-coloured worsted threads were dyed to resemble the original and the only difference the layman might notice is that the Reading Tapestry is in twenty-five sections, so that it can be sent out on loan exhibitions.

Archery is becoming an increasingly popular sport. Try to arrange a visit to see a demonstration.

CREATIVE ACTIVITIES
Writing
During a visit to Battle Abbey, write a 'dream' story of the events that took place there on October 25th, 1066.

Imagine you were a lookout at Pevensey and you watch the invasion fleet approaching over the horizon. Record your conversation with your companion.

You are on a Norman ship; write a song which includes a battle cry which everyone can repeat. If the class is learning French write the song in that language.

You are with Harold's army in the north when the word comes that the Normans are landing. Write a poem which tells of the forced march south. Use a map, and one of the reference books to note the route followed and the time taken. Prepare a rhythmic pattern of noise to use between each verse and as background—horses' hooves, marching feet, clanking armour and weapons.

Write a war correspondent's report on the battle and include interviews with the commanders, soldiers, and those wounded. Perhaps the local peasantry ?

Write a poem about the tapestry to use alongside art and craft work.

Write a story about life as a servant in a Norman castle on the day when William came to stay.

Write a poem about a Norman sword — how you found it, and who you think used it.

One section of *Conquest 1066* by Robert Furneaux, refers to the Conqueror's companions. Further information can be found in *They came with The Conqueror* by L. G. Pine. Refer to these lists to see if any child in the school has a name which appears there (or is very close to it) and try to research into his antecedents. Write about this study and the part played by the ancestor.

Drama and movement
Find out as much about the event, aspects which preceded it and the sequel. Talk about the situation and the character of the people involved.

Decide upon the sequence of events to be portrayed and consider how they will eventually be linked. Improvise dialogue and action with small groups of players, except for the battle scenes when the largest possible group will be involved. Keep most scenes reasonably short so that the action moves along quite rapidly.

Plan the battle scenes with great care, and without sound at first, emphasising the need for control of movement. When the pattern of movement has been decided upon, include weapons, armour, etc., and the shouting of commands. Finally allow natural expressions to be used along with other sounds of battle.

Listen to music suitable to illustrate various aspects of the story, e.g.
Saul by Handel (Funeral March).
Hamlet by Berlioz.
Great Gate of Kiev (Pictures — by Mussorgsky).
Eroica by Beethoven.
Coronation Anthem by Handel.

Take each part through the pageant with music, commentary and other effects (horses' hooves, swish of arrows, sound of the sea, marching feet. etc.). Then one final rehearsal with costume, armour, etc., and no stoppages.

Be prepared for bad weather and the possibility of having to do the whole thing indoors.

A sequence of events leading up to the coronation of William I.
Edward the Confessor talks to Harold about the succession.
Harold leaves England from Bosham, pausing to pray at the church.
Harold voyages to Normandy and is cast up on the shore.
He is apprehended by Guy of Ponthieu who takes him to Beaurain.
Messengers come from William demanding Harold's release.
After some parleying and insistence from William, the royal prisoner is escorted to Rouen.

Harold joins William in the siege of the cities of Dol and Dinan.

Harold is knighted by William and takes an oath of allegiance on a chest of holy relics (covered with a cloth until after the ceremony).

Harold returns to a cool reception from Edward, who is soon to die.
Harold assumes the kingship. He hears what his astrologers have to
say about the comet.

William's claim to the throne is refuted by Harold, and so the Norman
prepares an invasion fleet.

Enemies, Hardrada (King of Norway) and Tostig (his brother – deposed
ruler at Northumbria – and out of sympathy) await Harold at
Stamford Bridge and are defeated (25th September, 1066).

William sails from St. Valery, September 28th, 1066, with 10,000 plus
men and lands at Pevensey, unopposed.

William makes a camp at Hastings, gathers supplies, loots and murders
in the vicinity.

Harold hears the news of the invasion and travels south.
Battle positions taken up and conflict begins, ending in utter confusion
for the English and death for Harold and many other Englishmen.
March on London and eventual crowning of William in Westminster
Abbey.

Art

In the style of the Bayeux Tapestry, draw features of the story which
are not portrayed therein.

Draw a crayon picture of the Coronation of William at Westminster
Abbey.

Draw a picture of Harold hawking and paint it. Make up a simple
cardboard mounting frame for the portrait.

Refer to *Birds of Prey* by Glenys and Derek Lloyd (Hamlyn) and prepare
large silhouettes of all those birds used in hunting. Mount these on
small wood blocks against a suitable English countryside background.
Provide an identification key. (A visit to the Falconry at Newent in
Gloucestershire, the Museum at Tring, or the Natural History Museum
South Kensington would be valuable to make in this connection. The
film *Kes* to see the training of a kestrel, and the book *The Goshawk* by
T. H. White to see and read.)

In the Tapestry, there are 202 horses and mules, 55 dogs, 505 other animals. Examine a reproduction of the tapestry and create a bestiary – making a picture of each type of animal and adding it to a large panel.

Draw shields – round for the infantrymen and kite-shaped for the horsemen. Decorate these with various devices – dragons were popular. Heraldry did not come into being until the following century, but if this topic extends to embrace the whole of the Norman era, then this subject can be included with its special language and symbolism.

For reference:
Filmstrips: *Heraldry,* esp. No. 1 *Origins of Heraldry* (Visual Publications).
Books: *Simple Heraldry – cheerfully explained,* 1 Moncrieffe &
        D. Pottinger (Faber).
        Your book of Heraldry, Richard Slade (Faber).

Craft

Make a fabric panel selecting parts of the Bayeux Tapestry – use appliqué techniques with embroidery embellishments.

Make various weapons for use in the pageant. In most cases, handles need to be made of wood. Other items – axe-heads, sword handles, etc. can be made from stout card (in two identical pieces and fixed around the handle with sticky paper). Aluminium sprays may be found useful for the 'metal' parts of the weapons.

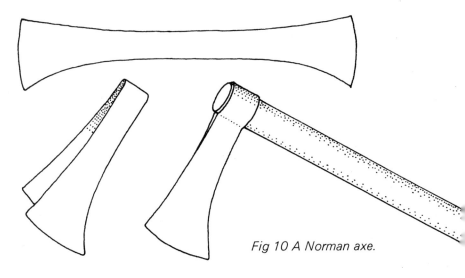

Fig 10 A Norman axe.

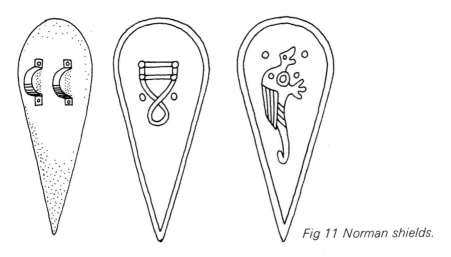

Fig 11 Norman shields.

Make a low relief sculpture of part of the Tapestry using Polystyrene.
Select a sheet which is half an inch thick. Draw out the section chosen,
using a felt-tipped pen. Leave all figures standing in relief by removing
a layer of the Polystyrene. This is done with the heated knob end of a
spare knitting needle or a knife blade. A small spirit lamp can be used to
heat the metal tools. Paint can now be applied and the title cut to the
desired shape.

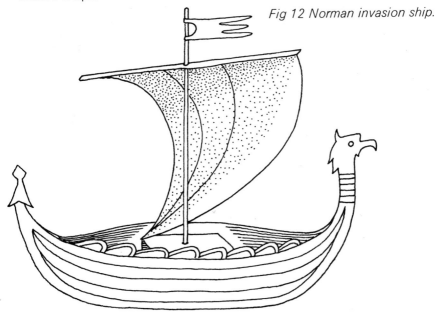

Fig 12 Norman invasion ship.

Look at the tapestry and make a fleet of Norman ships, complete with sails, mast and rigging, shields, soldiers and sailors. Cardboard and paper will be suitable materials. Double shapes of the boats should be drawn and joined together.at prow and stern with adhesive paper. A small block of wood or folded card should be fitted amidships to provide the three-dimensional effect.

Build the original Hastings castle, with a wooden palisade. Construct a Norman castle of later period using a large number of interlocked matchboxes. Leave one side open to reveal various floors and the activities carried on there. On a very large model, a spiral staircase can be shown in a partly opened tower. Matchboxes can be fixed around a central dowel rod with a cardboard strip to give this effect.

Make a model of the battlefield.
Choose a large board — preferable an Essex board or Sundeala. Look at a contour map of the battle area. Draw contours on the base board, lay a section of large-mesh chicken wire over the board and pull up the wire where there are hills. Near-accuracy can be achieved by erecting sticks cut to a suitable scale to represent spot heights or contour levels. Alternatively, layers of hardboard can be cut to represent each contour layer and these can be rested on blocks of wood cut to scale. (It is necessary to exaggerate the vertical scale three times in relation to the horizontal scale to make the hills worth looking at.)

Cover the wire, or hardboard contour layers, with pieces of muslin impregnated with plaster of Paris, or sheets of newspaper well covered with Polycell paste. When dry (half an hour with plaster or one day with Polycell) paint the battlefield, add such details as trees and bushes (with dyed cotton wool or sawdust.) Use small flags or painted blocks of wood to show the deployment of the two armies. (See the model of the battlefield in the Hastings Triodome.) Your model will be useful for briefing and tactical talk.

In schools where older boys study polymer science, effective models may be cast in plastics — see *Plastics for Schools* by P. J. Clarke (Mills and Boon).

Those who would like to re-enact the battle, might like to refer to *Charge, or How to Play War Games* by Brig. P. Young and Lt. Col.

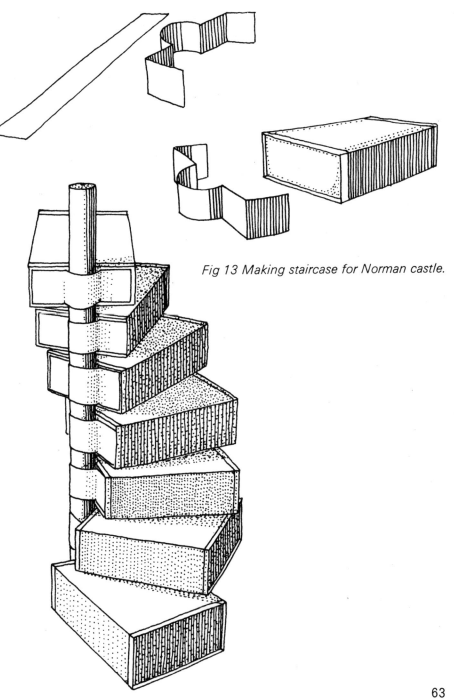

Fig 13 Making staircase for Norman castle.

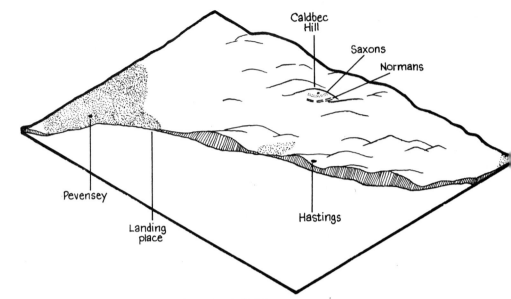

Fig 14 Model of Hastings battlefield area.

J. P. Lawford (Morgan Grampian) and *Naval War Games, War Games* and *Advanced War Games* by D. F. Featherstone (Stanley Paul) for advice on techniques and strategy.

Incidentally, metal figures of Normans can be purchased from Willie Figures, Edward Suren, 57 Ovington Street, London, S.W.3, and in plastic (and very much cheaper) from R. W. Spencer-Smith, 66 Long Meadow, Frimley, Nr. Camberley, Surrey.

Spear Pie was made annually to celebrate the events at Stamford Bridge. Invent a suitable pie for the Hastings Celebration.

Links with other celebrations
Trafalgar, Waterloo, Heights of Abraham, A battle near your own town.

A FESTIVAL OF GOOD NEIGHBOURS

It was Dr. Albert Schweitzer who said we should think occasionally of the suffering of which we spare ourselves the sight. In fact, there never has been such a time as this for reminding people of the needs of others. Pleas are made in newspapers, by post and on hoardings for help for those who are in a distressed condition. Statistics reveal that 12,000 people in the world will die TODAY of hunger, and that if we are average eaters then we will have consumed approximately 26 times more protein than the average Indian.

The period of Lent, which fits very conveniently into the half term just before Easter week, is appropriate for a Festival of Good Neighbours because week by week attention can be given to particular organisations, the work they do and what the children can do to help. Many of these groups have education departments and have produced many different types of aids to understanding the particular problems they have dedicated themselves to solving or at any rate relieving. If a varied treatment of the way of presentation is thought out each week, then there is little likelihood of boredom setting in.

Where churches, schools and other bodies have joined together locally to support a particular charitable work, then the individual efforts of one group can be the production of a festival to which others can be invited. Similarly the art and craft work of a number of schools can be brought together to form an exhibition with an appropriate film being shown. Visitors being asked to contribute something towards the funds will feel that they are better informed about the work which has to be done, while the children taking part will be in no doubt about the value of their effort if it is seen by many visitors.

Such a theme as this is one which can be made part of an Act of Worship, and to hold the act of celebration within a church would underline its importance for the children. We were able to enjoy the benefit of a good neighbour policy when the Head of the R.E. Department of our local comprehensive school accepted our invitation to accompany our singing on his guitar. This was a new experience for us, and the children responded well with their choral work.

Finally, the school in part or whole may wish to make a study of food supplies, or follow individual projects about children in particular countries, and at the end bring their work together on exhibition.

Plate 3 Reviewing the situation – The Artful Dodger and Fagin. Surprisingly enough the Good Neighbours Festival. (Kentish Times Photograph)

SOURCES OF INFORMATION
Books

The Hungry World, Elizabeth Stamp (Arnolds).
The World Must Eat (United Nations Study Guide).
Cry Humanity, Janet Lacey (S.C.M. Press).
Who Is My Neighbour? edited Esther Pike (Seabury Press USA).
Royal Maundy (Pitkin Pictorial Series).
Series of books from Methuen Press, e.g. *Bala, Child of India,* from Chatto and Windus, *Parana* (from Brazil), and from Hutchinson, *Children of the Highlands.*
For God's Sake Care, Salvation Army (Constable).

Songs

When I Needed a Neighbour
Fair Shares For All
The Family of Man
Feed Us Now
Half The World
Dives and Lazarus
If I had a Hammer. All to be found in *Faith Folk and Clarity* (Galliard Press)
Last Night I had the Strangest Dream
The Jericho Road
Good King Wenceslas
All You Need Is Love (Lennon and McCartney)
Consider Yourself at Home (Lionel Bart)
Do As You Would Be Done By (Leslie Bricusse and Cyril Ornadel from Pickwick)
Who Is My Neighbour (recorded on EMI 33SX 1609, A Man Dies)
Brotherhood Of Man (from 'How to Succeed in Business without Really Trying' and recorded on RCA Victor RD 7564)

Films

The Vicious Spiral, Christian Aid.
A Developing Man, Oxfam.
Half of Mankind, Contemporary Films.
The World's Need, Oxfam.
Food or Famine, Petroleum Films Bureau.
The Hungry Ones, Oxfam.
Tractor on the Ocean, Christian Aid.
Oliver Twist, Rank Films.

Other aids

Oxfam: 274 Banbury Road, Oxford. (Charts, project folders, photographs news sheets, fact sheets, films, etc.).

Christian Aid: P.O. No. 1. London S.W.1. (Annual reports on work projects, films, filmstrips, tape recordings, slides, posters, assembly suggestion leaflets.)

Voluntary Committee on Overseas Aid and Development (V.C.O.A.D.): 69, Victoria Street, London, S.W.1. (Co-ordinated service on

information and aids available from most organisations.)
Shelter, National Campaign for the Homeless: 86, The Strand, London, W.C.2. (Newsheet on work in hand – various local campaign literature.)
Help The Aged: Room T1 139 Oxford Street, London, W.1.
Save The Children Fund: 29 Queen Anne's Gate, London, S.W.1. (Quarterly Magazine about SCF work.)
War on Want: 9 Madeley Road, London, W.5.
UNICEF: New Gallery Centre, 123 Regent Street, London, W.1.
Catholic Institute for International Relations: 38 King Street, London W.C.2.
Freedom From Hunger Campaign: 17 Northumberland Avenue, London, W.C.2.
Christian Education Movement: Annandale, North End Road, London, N.W.11.
Council for Education in World Citizenship: 93 Albert Embankment, London, S.E.1.
Salvation Army: 101 Queen Victoria Street, P.O. Box 249, London, E.C.4.
Dr Barnardo's Homes: 18 Stepney Causeway, London, E.1.
British Red Cross Society: 14/15 Grosvenor Crescent, London, S.W.1.
Pestalozzi Children's Village Trust: 81 High Street, Battle, Sussex.

Excursions
To local exhibitions featuring the work of any of the above organisations. Commonwealth Institute, Kensington, London.
Where immigrants have built up a large community, they will celebrate their mother country's national day, etc. We made a request to visit a Woolwich celebration of Indian National Day, and our party were received with enthusiasm by everyone, and enjoyed hearing and watching songs and dances by native performers.

CREATIVE ACTIVITIES
Written work
Choose a country overseas and produce a biography of a boy or girl; how they live, what they eat; what work their parents do; interesting local customs and pastimes; etc.

Use a local newspaper and find information about people in your town who are in need of help. Write down what could be done.

Read a national daily paper or watch the next news bulletin to learn of a disaster or accident which has occurred. Write a poem about the problem.

Make a list of all the voluntary bodies in your town and arrange to interview a representative to discover what particular area of need they cover.

Choose a food product and carry out research into various sources of information about it, with a personal report at the end of the study (Christian Aid's project leaflet *Your Cup of Tea* will suggest a format to try – and with an interesting end of project get-together to consider the plight of some less fortunate neighbours.)

Ask everyone to provide their definition of a neighbour, and gather these together, with illustrations – amusing and poignant, where possible.

A good neighbour . . . helps a child across a road.
gives money to charity
is a fireman
is somebody who sticks by you when you're in trouble
who looks after your children when you have another one
who'll cook the food when you're ill
who'll keep you company when you're lonely.

Write a story of someone who was a good neighbour to your family.

Read *World Of The Child* (Penguin Books) in which the written comments of a North London Primary School are complemented by pictures of their British situation and these are contrasted with scenes and descriptions of children from deprived countries. Try a similar project, using hand-out material from organisations listed in this section.

Write a class ballad appropriate to the theme.

Here is an example which was produced during our Festival – our accompanist provided the music (see page 175), but a natural extension would be the setting of the poem to music by the children using tuned percussion.

Who Cares? Who Cares?

Who cares in this world, who cares?
Who cares in this world who cares?
Who cares for the dying?
Who cares for the sick?
Who cares in this world, who cares?

Who cares for the poor, who cares?
Who cares for the poor who cares?
Who cares for the hungry?
Who cares for the weak?
Who cares for the poor who cares?

Who cares about war, who cares?
Who cares about war, who cares?
Who cares about killing?
Who cares about suffering?
Who cares about war, who cares?

We care in this world, we care
We care in this world, we care
We care for the dying,
We care for the sick.
We care for you all, we care.

Drama and movement

Read the story of the Good Samaritan. Dramatise the parable. Create a modern parallel to the story.

Read *The General* by Janet Charters and Michael Foreman (Routledge and Kegan Paul). Act this story of General Jodpur who made himself the most famous commander in the world, by banning war.

Create the dramatic situation of the supporters of the home team who react badly to the visitors who come to see their team play . . . and how the referee resolves the conflict. Use *West Side Story* music for movement sequences.

In the 12th century, members of a noble family in Whitby killed a priest who refused to admit them to church after boar hunting. Before he died the priest persuaded the Abbot to be merciful to his slayers. The punishment, still carried on by the descendant of the Percy, Bruce and Abbotson families today, is to build a Penny (Penitent) Hedge of stakes which has to withstand the force of three tides. This ceremony is carried out on Ascension Eve on Boyes Staith Sands, Whitby. Sir Walter Scott brings this story into his poem *Marmion.* Improvise this story.

At Tichborne in Hampshire on Lady Day, the annual dole of bread is given out to the poor. This ceremony has gone on since the 12th century when the lord of the manor agreed to give his wife as much land as she could encircle before her firebrand burnt out. She rose from her sick bed and managed to drag herself around $23\frac{1}{2}$ acres (still known as The Crawls). The produce from this acreage provided flour for the parish poor. Develop this story and perform it.

Perform part or all of *Oliver Twist* (with or without music from Lionel Bart).

Find out all you can about St. Martin and the beggar and act this episode as a mime.

During the Great Plague of 1665 and 1666, the infection spread to the Derbyshire village of Eyam. The villagers responded to the pleas of their rector, William Mompesson, and imposed self-imprisonment on themselves. In all, 260 of them died, but the plague did not pass over the parish boundaries. Food was left for them by a stone. Here at Rock Pulpit, on the last Sunday in August, Plague Sunday, an open air service is held. (Refer to Sutherland Ross's book the *Plague and the Fire* for further details.) Prepare a play of this story.

Adapt a dance or create a new one called the Good Neighbours Get Together, in which there are various courtesies like hand-shaking and moving in a large circle. Use various instruments to suggest different cultures — African, Oriental, etc.

Art and Craft
Make up simple doll shapes and dress them in national costume.

Make up a frieze of children of different lands, all joining hands around a map of the world.

Make a series of models showing farming methods in different parts of the world.

72

Make up an emaciated figure – clad only in loin cloth – as the Universal Unknown Refugee. Use wire or cane for the armature and 'clothe' with papier mâché.

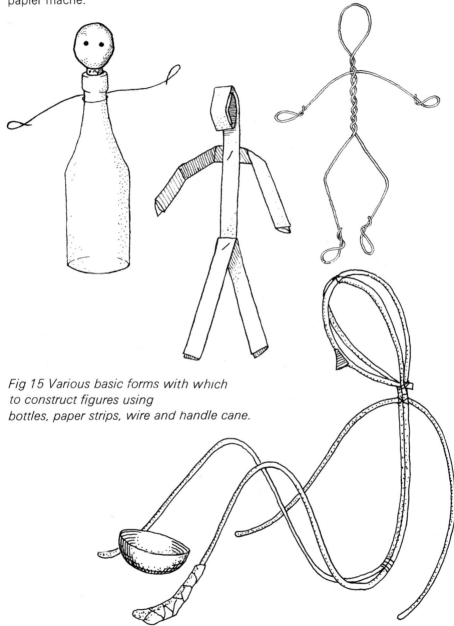

Fig 15 Various basic forms with which
to construct figures using
bottles, paper strips, wire and handle cane.

Make a model showing the events of a recent tragedy – earthquake, volcanic eruption, flooding, war, etc. Add relief workers to the model after it has been on display for a few days.

Make up a number of puppets for use in the Story of the Good Samaritan.

Draw and colour a picture of a lifeboat rescue. Acrylic paints can be tried to provide an interesting texture for the sea and sky.

Links with other festivals
Children's Day; a local charity; United Nations' Celebration; Peace.

A TONGAN CELEBRATION

In an earlier chapter, the reason for the selection of this tiny group of islands as the central theme for a school festival has been explained. Since only a very short time was available, the efforts of the whole school were concentrated upon this single enterprise. In normal circumstances, one class might have adopted that country and joined with other classes, studying neighbouring islands and countries, in holding a Festival of the Pacific. This section, therefore, may be found useful as a pattern for a larger festival.

INFORMATION AND INSPIRATION
Books
Certain publications are suggested which give a regional treatment of the subject.
Bain, Kenneth: *The Friendly Islanders* (Hodder and Stoughton).
Kennedy, T. F.: *Farmers of the Pacific Islands* (A. H. & A. W. Reed, NZ – obtainable from the Commonwealth Institute).
Mead, Margaret: *Growing up in New Guinea* and *Coming of age in Samoa* (Penguin).
Reed, W. W.: *Tonga* (Warne – Children's Social Study Reader).
Rosedal, Jorgen: *The Happy Lagoons* (Jarrolds).
Westphal, Fritz: *Tongan Tabu* (Methuen).
National Geographic Magazine March 1968 issue for two well-illustrated articles (N.G. Magazine, 11 Stanhope Gate, London, W.1)
Macquarie, Hector: *The Friendly Queen* (Heinemann).

Other aids
Filmstrips: *Tonga* (Hulton Press – on loan from Commonwealth Institute).
           The South Sea Islands (Visual Information Services).
Films: *The Royal visit to Fiji and Tonga* (Rank Films).
           People of Paradise – Royal Tonga (BBC Enterprises).
Record: *Music of Tonga* (Viking, VP 108).
Leaflets: *The Coconut* and *Groundnuts* (Commonwealth Institute).

Useful addresses
Commonwealth Friendship Movement, 25 Longhill Road, Ovingdean, Brighton 7.
VCOAD, Education Unit, 69 Victoria Street, London, S.W.1.
New Zealand House, Haymarket, London, S.W.1.

Music

Tongan National Anthem (Koe Fasi Oe Tu'i Oe Otu Toga).

Nature Carol – arrangement by Sir Malcolm Sargent of a Polynesian song. This was used in a BBC Singing Together programme some years ago. For the words of this and the anthem, the BBC were most helpful.

Methodist & Wesleyan hymns – taken there by the missionaries more than a century ago, e.g. *God Be With You Till We Meet Again.*

CREATIVE ACTIVITIES
Written work

You are a young fisherman, out to catch your first octupus. Tell of your adventures. (See Sir Arthur Grimble's account of just such a venture in *A Pattern of Islands.*)

(The octopus fishermen chant as they fish

Octopus, descending fast
Octopus descending fast
Spotted one come, spotted one come
Come hither one, come hither two
Come hither into the boat.

and a lure of crab meat is dangled over the side of the boat.)

Tin Can Island in the Tongan group got its name because the mail had to be put into tin cans and thrown overboard for a brave swimmer to collect. Write a poem about this, and set it to music – with a Tongan beat to it.

Imagine that you attended the coronation of King Taufa'ahau Tupou IV on Tuesday, July 4th, 1967. Describe the ceremony and the feast and celebrations afterwards.

Drama and movement

Learn a Polynesian Dance and perform it to music.

Captain James Cook was the first Englishman to visit Tonga, 1733. After looking up details of this landing and naming of the place – The Friendly Islands – recreate the story.

The legend of the Island of Tonga. Tongamatamoa was a great God of the Heavens. He sent his only daughter to earth but when she grew up into a beautiful maiden her protective father spirited her back again. All the men attempted to find her and perished in the attempt – all save two, Maui Kisikisi, and his brother Maui Atalanga. They found the hidden pathway and with the help of kindly spirits on the way, they overcame all temptations of food and arrived at the heavenly palace. There they were welcomed and fed. The great god then asked them which fish hook they would like to have. The princess had advised them to select the old and worn hook, and this they did. It was the right one – the only one fit to catch the great fish, the Bonito. With this hook, they pulled up from the deepest part of the ocean a piece of land which they called Tongatapu – or sacred Tonga, then another, and another, until the whole archipelago was on the surface of the ocean – and it was all called Tonga. Perform this legend.

History's most famous mutiny took place near the islands of Tofua and Kao on April 28th, 1789. Enact the incident when Captain William Bligh and his loyal crewmen were set adrift by Fletcher Christian.

Art
Make a picture showing the men of Tonga fishing at sunset with harpoons and carrying a blazing branch to dazzle the prey.

Make a large picture showing dancers in national costume. Use tissue paper of various colours to make skirts and other decorations, for wrists, necks, ankles and heads.

Draw a treasure map of the islands.

Craft
Make a model of a Tongan island, with single room huts, fishing boats, etc.

Make a mobile using the shape of the flying squirrel.

Part of the Tongan group is volcanic. Using cardboard and papier mâché, make up a volcano model. Cotton wool and steel wool suspended over the crater will simulate smoke. Acrylic paint of various colours painted on the side of the volcano can be sprinkled with ash to represent flowing lava.

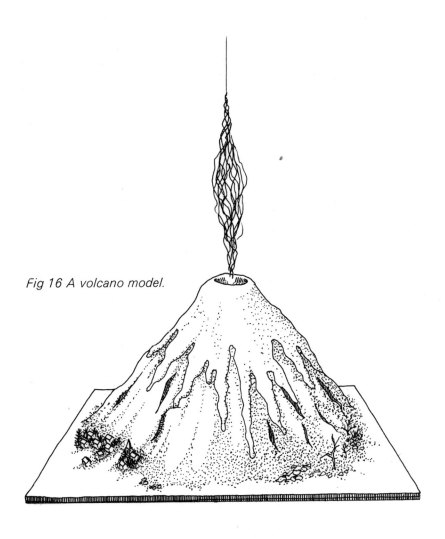

Fig 16 A volcano model.

Tapa cloth is made by pounding water-soaked mulberry bark into thin strips, which are joined together into large sheets using the juice of the manioc root. Various plates are made for printing and these are prepared by sewing fibres and roots onto a leaf base. The tapa cloth is then placed over a cylinder of wood to which the plates have been added. A dye is then applied to the areas of the cloth raised up by the designs on the plates. Drying takes place in the sun. Strips of cardboard, twigs, roots or thin pieces of wood can be laid onto a piece of hardboard or stout card and glued into position. Cloth or paper can now be placed

Fig 17 A design for tapa cloth.

over the plates, and crayons or paint should be rubbed over the raised designs to make texture relief patterns.

(Pieces of tapa cloth can be purchased from Eatons, Manette Street, London, W.1. Also shells, and corals from the Pacific.)

Make an attractive arrangement of products and materials associated with Tonga. Ask the greengrocer (with early warning of requirements) for coconuts (and desiccated coconut), sweet potatoes, yams, taro, cassava, groundnuts, candlenuts, bananas, pineapple, melons, mangoes, citrus fruits.

Coir rope, stamps from the island, a coin, tapa cloth, coral and shells can also be collected.

Make up dancing skirts from the Pacific, using lengths of raffia.
Make up a dancing skirt using Vilene or similar material.

Using a coconut shell, cut and polish a shape for a drinking cup for ceremonial kava drinking.

Use coconut fibres and a piece of stick to manufacture a flywhisk.

Tuimalilu was one of the great tortoises, seen by Captain Cook in 1770. It died in 1966. Make a model of this animal.

Using tissue paper, make up flower shapes and join these together as garlands.

Links with other festivals
Another island people – Malta, Tristan da Cunha, Isle of Man, Arran, etc.

A FESTIVAL OF THE STREET

If for no other reason, such a celebration could be arranged to focus attention on road safety. To learn that any child born in this decade has a fifty per cent chance of being involved in a road accident, is enough to make one seek for new ways of instructing the young.

It is surely an advantage to draw from the current work of the class, material which could be used directly in a festival. The street as a theme was assured of interested involvement with several of the classes who were following various projects. Thus the group studying South-East Asia were able to portray a Hong Kong street with all its colour and bustle. A team-teaching centre of interest was the Medieval Times and they presented a day in a town street of 1400. This contrasted with an older class topic on the Victorians, and with the help of photographs of Mr. Spurgeon's Greenwich on exhibition at the local library and loaned

Plate 4 "Who will buy my sweet red roses?"
(*Kentish Times Photograph*)

to us, the children were able to give us a realistic picture of our borough almost a century ago. Another class had been studying the mathematical aspects of our estate and the results of their observations and calculations were illustrated and described to the audience.

In the research into this kind of project one stumbles across some interesting reading. *Two Lamps in Our Street – A Time Remembered* by Arthur Barton (New Authors Ltd.) and *Share My Taxi* by Robert Buckland (Michael Joseph) were two nostalgic autobiographies I enjoyed reading.

SOURCES OF INFORMATION
Books
Singing Street, James T. R. Ritchie (Oliver and Boyd).
Children's Games in Street and Playground, Iona and Peter Opie (Oxford).
Play in Childhood, Margaret Lowenfeld (Gollancz).
Traditional Games in England – 2 vols., Scotland and Ireland, A. B. Gomme (Constable Dover).
The Open Road, H. J. Deverson and Ronald Lampitt (Oxford).
The Roadmakers, L and J. Havenhand (Wills and Hepworth).
The Story of British Roads, British Road Federation.
Man and Roads, E. Cowrie (Hamish Hamilton).
How Roads Have Grown, P. Rush (Routledge and Kegan Paul).
Mayhew's London, Mayhew's Characters, London's Underworld, Henry Mahew (Spring Books).
Policemen and the Police Force, H. Adams (Blackwell).
London's Pavement Pounders, Geoffrey Fletcher (Hutchinson).
Looking at London, Ronald Searle and Kaye Webb (News Chronicle).
Signs in Action, James Sutton (Studio Vista).
The Highway Code (HMSO).

Poetry
Rum Lane, James Reeves.
The Deserted House, Mary Coleridge.
In Campbell Street, Rosemary Winn.
The Song of the Roadbuilders, Ewan MaColl.
Hide and Seek, Vernon Scannell.

Music
An interesting selection can be taken from various films and shows which have already been learnt for sheer pleasure from radio and record even where the actual performance has not been seen.

Feed the Birds (from *Mary Poppins*).
Standing on the corner (from *Most Happy Fella*).
On the street where you live (from *My Fair Lady*).
In Montmarte (from *Can-Can*).
Who will buy? (from *Oliver*).
Past three o'clock, Have you seen the muffin man? and *Cockles and mussels* are examples of older songs to include.
Street Cries and *The Streets of London* (Argo ZDA 47).
Street Corner Overture, Alan Rawsthorne (Pye GGC 4048).
Children's Overture, Roger Quilter.
Music of the streets – a record of mechanical street music (Saydisc).
Children's Singing Games (Topic, Imp. A 101 – book available).
Johnny Crack (from *Under Milk Wood* – Dylan Thomas).

Films

Morning in the streets (BBC Films Enterprises).
Mathematics and The Village (1. Shape, 2. Number, 3. Measurement – Rank Films).
Boy Goes Cycling (Company of Veteran Motorists).
Bouncing Fellow (Royal Society for Prevention of Accidents).
Just Threepence (ROSPA).
Trouble in Toytown (ROSPA).
Meet the Foresights (Company of Veteran Motorists).
The Ballad of the battered bicycle (PFB).
Giuseppina (BP Films).
Highway Assignment (Vauxhall Motors Ltd. from Rank Films).

Excursions

Into the street in different parts of the town or city to investigate street names, architecture, shops, particular features, traffic census, accident black spots, etc.
Royal Society for the prevention of Accidents, Terminal House, Knightsbridge, London W.1.
Museums, e.g. Transport Museum, Clapham; Science Museum, South Kensington, London for transport sections and displays on street lighting, fire prevention, etc.
Transport Museum, Belfast; Brighton Motor Museum; Beaulieu Motor Museum; Cheddar Motor Museum; Museum of Carriages, Maidstone; Crich Tramway Museum, Derbyshire; Transport Museum, Hull, as well as most others which will include certain aspects of roads and transportation.

Visit places where street facades are strictly controlled – Bath, Brighton, etc.

Other aids

Record: *The London Tram,* Argo EAF 142 and 143.
Privately taken slides – to open some eyes to what there is in the street.
Quarterly magazine: *Safe Training,* ROSPA.
Road accident statistics from local police.
Leaflet: *Notes on the Cries of London,* London Museum, Kensington Palace.
Demonstration: Invite police into playground to give a road safety display to coincide with the festival.
Alternative programme for indoors – talk with slides; the National Cycling Proficiency Scheme can be introduced; pictures of street scenes, e.g. Brueghel's *Children's Games;* L. S. Lowry's *Street in Clitheroe;* a Giles cartoon.

CREATIVE ACTIVITIES
Written work

Use a portable tape recorder to gather sound effects from a local shopping area or market. Note highlights over fifteen minutes. Write cameo sketches of these incidents and punctuate with sound effects already recorded.

Arrange to start early in the morning, with written permission from parents, to record details of the street coming alive. Take photographs or transparencies of the different scenes.

Produce a classbook of people of the street in various categories (a) street labourers, (b) street sellers and buyers, (c) street workers –. policemen, postmen, etc. (d) street entertainers, (e) street evangelists, and politicians, (f) society problems. (Tape recorded interviews, photographs, sketches, etc.)

Write a poem describing your street on a rainy day.

Write a story about the day the gas board, electricity council and water authority all decided to dig up your street.

Write a ballad about a hold-up at the local High Street bank.

Prepare some slogans and thoughts for the Wayside Pulpit.

Collect the names of inns and hotels in the town and write a story about one of them.

Write a cautionary tale about a boy or girl who almost becomes involved in a series of accidents.

Write a road safety song with a refrain line reminding everyone of their kerb drill.

Drama and movement
Carry out research into the social scene of particular eras in history – Roman times, Middle Ages, the Elizabethans, Georgian period, etc. Produce sequence of actions and conversations which will illustrate the social conditions of the times, e.g. a carrier is bringing a supply of Dorset stone for the new cathedral gateway in 1400. He leaves a wheel at the smith to repair; refreshes himself at the inn; listens to a travelling priest; buys some material for his wife, talks to the lay brothers at the abbey. A policeman might act as the link for a Victorian scene, and a window-cleaner for today's street.

Listen to market traders selling their wares today, compare with past cries. Make up some new ones selling the wares of today's tradesmen. Open up your street of shops and try to attract customers.

Gather details of songs, games and activities from the playground and street, and build together into a sequence. Focal point of attention gained by speech, action and movement towards the centre of acting area. Here is a brief description of a unit we called Mathematics of the Street, and which was created to be presented separately as the light relief for a mathematics conference.

Tape-record section from Quilter's *Children's Overture* – fading out during *Boys and Girls Come Out To Play* – sounds of an isolated car – first bus – with conductor's ring, motorbike – cock crowing – church clock ringing 7 – then milkman's vehicle, and rattle of milk bottles. (Cock crowing and church bell from sound effects records, other material gathered live.) Child refers to early morning scene, scathing comment about the motor-cyclist, waking everyone up, tells us it is Saturday morning and the milkman is delivering his milk and collecting his money.

The action is now carried on as the milkman comes in and deals with two customers. Group of skipping girls move in, carrying out individual activity and then collective skipping. (*I know a boy who is double jointed, Vote vote vote for dear old Wendy? Archibald, bald, bald, Mother's in the kitchen,* etc., etc.

A game of conkers then takes over — interrupted by a postman who reminisces as he empties the postbox. Game of *What's the Time Mr. Wolf?* followed by some cat's cradle work with string loops. Children come in and play a game of Jacks, followed by a sequence in which top spinning and the playing with a yo-yo go on, interrupted by bartering between two people, which then gives place to a game of hop scotch. A rag and bone man then temporarily spoils their game by going across it, and persuades a householder to part with lots of woollens for a modest gift. A newsboy now adds his voice to the proceedings and everyone joins in. The exit is achieved by the tape-recorded sound of thunder and rain.

Enact the story of the Street Arab's friend, Dr. Barnardo.

Collect a number of group games and songs and prepare a sequence for the youngest children.

Plan a series of episodes, loosely based upon the *Coronation Street* serial on I.T.V. If some uplifting note can be struck in each sequence, these productions could be used for a series of assemblies, e.g. the need for rules of the road; the cutting down of a much-loved tree to make way for road widening; litter in the street; why we need a police force, etc.

Young children will enjoy taking part in a fancy dress parade of street people.

Busker entertainment with home-made instruments and properties.

Art and craft
Involve a large group of children in the preparation of a backcloth for the celebration, showing a shopping street.

Design some modern shop signs and contrast with traditional ones. Make a collage picture of a Pearly King and Queen — a school collection of buttons will be necessary.

88

Do-it-yourself pavement pictures in chalk.

Produce some designs for new lamp standards – and then model in balsa wood.

Produce a series of card models showing the development of transport through the ages.

Make sketches of local streets and then model these in cardboard. Use manufactured car models.

Model a street accident.

Divide into small groups and walk the streets gathering details of length, number of houses, lamp-posts, telephone boxes, etc. Produce a large-scale map of the district with this information added.

Plan an excursion to discover all the shapes in the surrounding streets.

Draw a seedy street and then give it a Civic Design facelift.

Make up a montage of road safety signs (such a task can be made the subject of a competition).

Model the area surrounding the school, with streets clearly marked. Indicate with coloured threads the routes followed by different children as they travel from home to school.

Make life-size models of various items of street furniture – police call box, postbox, etc.

Create a frieze in which the seasonal changes in the street are illustrated; snow clearance, Easter parade, off for the holidays, ice cream, conkers, Guy Fawkes, carol singing, Christmas shops, etc.

Links with other celebrations
The river, the seaside.

A FESTIVAL OF THE ZODIAC

To judge by the number of daily newspapers and weekly magazines which employ a regular astrologer, there is a tremendous interest in forecasts about one's future prospects. There is probably no need to say, however, that most of these 'forecasts' are so general that they become totally useless and it might be a good idea to warn children against superstitions of this nature.

References to such publications as *Your Character in the Zodiac* by Rupert Gleadow (Phoenix), *Teach Yourself Astrology* (English Universities Press), *Astrology*, Louis MacNeice (Aldus), *Astrology* by Astarte (Bancroft), *Stars of Fortune*, Cynthia Harnett (Methuen), *Horoscopes*, Which Magazine June 1969, will provide explanations and insight into this most ancient of sciences.

At Boxgrove school, we seek to celebrate on a day in mid-summer and look back on the year's achievements. A distinguished speaker is invited and after a short speech, we get down to the serious business of entertaining our visitors and ourselves. As many people as possible are involved in the occasion and the intention is to give enjoyment but at the same time to explore the realms of music, movement, drama, poetry and prose, etc. The entertainment may well be linked with some national or local celebration, special occasion for the school, or a theme explored in the head teacher's report. That year the 'Message' was that pleasant as it was to look backwards, it was imperative that we look forward too – and perhaps the stars could provide the answer. So the zodiac was adopted as the festival theme, and each group was asked to provide some creative activity which would illustrate their sign of the zodiac. I propose for this section to describe the programme under zodiacal symbols.

Selections of music used to introduce items and provide interludes were *The Planets' Suite* by Gustav Holst, *Horoscope* by Constant Lambert. The various movements in this ballet are *Dance for the Followers of Leo, Sarabande for the Followers of Virgo, Valse for the Followers of Gemini, Bacchanale for the Followers of Leo, Invocation to the Moon and Finale.* Also *Gemini Variations* by Benjamin Britten (Decca SXL 6264). The programme can be introduced by the March of the Royal Air Force and an introductory poem could be selected from one of the following: *Looking at Stars*, Phoebe Hasketh, *Startalk*, Robert Graves, *The Zodiac*, Eleanor Farjeon.

Aries
The Ram, March 21st–April 20th
Song: The Derby Ram with an enormous picture of the beast.

Taurus
The Bull, April 21st–May 22nd
Play: The story of the Minotaur and the Labyrinth of King Minos.

Gemini
The Twins, May 23rd–June 21st
Play: A story written by twins in the school who by their identical appearance were able to outwit the teacher and so take half a day off school per day. They wrote a highly moral ending.

Cancer
The Crab, June 22nd–July 23rd
Movement: Low Tide on the seashore – music from *Facade* by William Walton.

Leo
The Lion, July 23rd–August 22nd
Play: *Androcles and the Lion.*

Virgo
The Maiden, August 23rd–September 22nd
Play: *Europa and the Bull.* (At a Roman villa nearby there is a splendid mosaic of this legend, which was reproduced as a paper square mosaic with seasonal symbols at each corner.)

Libra
The Scales, September 23rd–October 22nd
A story – mimed. In fact this story illustrates the law which we all learn at some time in physics, that a floating body loses in weight an amount equal to that of the liquid displaced. Archimedes leapt from his bath on realising this and ran through the streets of Syracuse yelling 'Eureka!'. The second part of the story illustrates the practical application of this principle when a dishonest goldsmith tried to adulterate a crown of gold for King Hieron by adding silver to it. Achimedes was able to expose the villain and have him punished – by using his scales.

Scorpio
The Scorpion, October 23rd–November 21st
Dance: the courtship of the scorpions to the music of an American
square dance (an idea 'borrowed' from Walt Disney's film
The Vanishing Prairie).

Sagittarius
The Archer, November 22nd–December 22nd
Folk tale: William Tell with the music overture *William Tell* by Rossini.

Capricorn
The Goat, December 23rd–January 20th
Play and song: *Three Billy Goats Gruff*. This was performed by a
transition class.

Aquarius
The Water Carrier, January 21st–February 19th
Song and movement: *The Age of Aquarius* (from *Hair*).

Pisces
The Fish, February 20th–March 20th
Underwater ballet sequence with music, *Carnival of the Animals*
(The Aquarium) by Saint Saens. Children were in bathing costumes
with raffia trimmings. The wallbars and PE apparatus were in use to
provide a three-dimensional area for movement (preceding Peter
Brook's interpretation of *Midsummer Night's Dream* at Stratford 1970).
Spotlights with green and blue filters provided sub-aquamarine
colouring.

The hall was marked out into the zodiacal areas and at key points
within them, the signs and symbols of each were displayed. From a book
of astrology, some general pointers to the character of those born
within specific periods were summarised – two favourable factors and
one detrimental. A reading of each – with all in the group standing –
punctuated the performance. Far more shock was registered when one
saw who else one shared the same fate and fortune with, than in
learning what it was to be! A new series – Occultia – has been issued
by the Marble Arch recording company. I listened to the *Fortunes of
Aquarius* (MAL 1310) and learnt much to my advantage. I was told
that I ought to choose my soul-mate from the Gemini group – what a
pity I didn't know that before!

In writing and music-making, there are obviously many opportunities for the development of ideas stimulated by the zodiac. In starting to develop a tune on chime bars, the various animals involved might be a good starting point, with their character, 'voice', mode of travel, explored. The watery aspect of Aquarius and the twin factors of Gemini are places to commence the work.

Links with other festivals
Magic and Mystery; Space, Astronomy and Science; The Seasons; The Year.

THE FEAST OF ST. VALENTINE

During the controversy which raged about the showing of filmstrips and television programmes about sex education, what seemed to be missing was much reference to love. So we might say that this celebration on February 14th is more about the Facts of Love and less about the Facts of Life.

Believing in the equality of the sexes, Boxgrove held its festival in a leap year. The shape of the heart, adopted as the symbol for the whole occasion (it would be preferable to 'affair') was marked out in masking tape and so defined the arena and symbolised the theme.

INFORMATION AND INSPIRATION
Books
Brown, Ivor: ed. *A Book of Marriage* (Hamish Hamilton).
Dupont, Paul: *Across a Crowded Room* (Leslie Frewen).
Jay, Antony: ed. *The Pick of the Rhubarb* (Hodder and Stoughton) for some interesting sections, e.g. Pop the Question, The Kiss, First Love, Till Death Us Do Part, and even The Coy Virtue, May and December, the Sex War and The Brush Off.
Shaw, Bernard: *Prefaces* and the plays, *Getting Married, Candida, Man and Superman.*
Staff, *The Valentine and its origins* (Lutterworth) and *Valentines* (Castle Museum, York).

Poetry
Betjeman, John: *From a Surrey Garden.*
Browning, Elizabeth: *How do I love thee?*
Brooke, Rupert: *The Chilterns.*
Burns, Robert: *Highland Mary, My love is like a red, red rose.*
Byron, Lord: *She walks in beauty; Oh, talk not to me.*
Emerson: *Give all to love.*
Heywood, Thomas: *Pack clouds away, and welcome day.*
Hopkins, Kenneth: *Most gracious are the gestures of her hands.*
Jonson, Ben: *To Celia* (Drink to me only with thine eyes).
Longfellow, H. W.: *Hiawatha's Wedding Feast.*
Moore, Thomas: *The Young May is beaming.*
Rosetti, Christina: *My heart is like a singing bird.*
Scott, Sir W.: *The sun upon the lake is low.*
Shakespeare, William: *Live with me, and be my love; It was a lover and his lass; Shall I compare thee to a summer's day?*
Tennyson, A. O.: *O let the solid ground* (from *Maud*).

Wordsworth, William: *She was a phantom of delight.*
The Song of Solomon, 1,15; *Behold thou art fair, my love.*
Yeats, W. B.: *Down by the Sally Gardens.*
Love poems of the 16th and 17th centuries – Argo records EAF 44
and 45.

Songs and other music

Love has occupied the attentions of composers since Adam and Eve
probably so there is no shortage of music to use.

Classical
Mendelsohn, F.: *Midsummer Night's Dream.*
Tchaikovsky, P.: Overture to *Romeo and Juliet.*

Folk and traditional songs
*Billy Boy; Bobby Shafto; The Drummer and the Cook; Lavender's Blue;
The Farmer's Daughter; The Girl with the Jet Black Hair; Madam,
Madam; O, No John; O Soldier, Soldier; Sweet Polly Oliver; The Wee
Cooper of Fife; Greensleeves; The Keys of Heaven; A-Roving;
A Frog he would a-wooing go.*
Listen to Songs of Courtship, Topic 12 T157.

Opera
The Bird Catcher's Song (Mozart's *Magic Flute*).
Your tiny hand is frozen (Puccini's *La Bohème*).

Stage and screen
*Daisy, Daisy; There was I waiting at the church; Get me to the church
on time.*

Light opera
When a merry maiden marries; Take a pair of sparkling eyes (The
Gondoliers); *Twenty love sick maidens we; Prithee pretty maiden*
(Patience); *Brightly dawns our wedding day* (The Mikado).

French
Plaisir d'Amour; La vie en rose.

Pop songs
Just turn the radio on.

Excursions

A wedding service in a local church, after asking for permission.
Additional possibilities here are a tape recording, slides and an 8 mm
movie film of the service for later use in class.

CREATIVE ACTIVITIES
Written work

Compose a valentine in any vein you like:

Is thy heart from anguish free
Dost thou ever think of me
Doth my lass to love incline
Will she be my Valentine?

My love is like a cabbage
Divided into two
The leaves I give to others
But the heart I give to you.

Or it can be in the form of a cryptic word puzzle written on a particular
shape of paper – in the example given – it was a glove.

```
I   NT  ALK IN  GLOVES  APL EASI  NGTH  EME
I   NSLE EPIN GLOVES   AHE AVE  NL  YDRE  AM
INF IG  HTIN GLOVES   ITS EL  FSAH OS  T
IND RINK IN  GLOVES   TH  EFAV OR  ITETO AST
```

Or write a couplet in the form of a question, and invite someone else
to compose the last two lines in reply.

Write the story of one of the songs in the music list.

Prepare definitions of LOVE and HATE; a LAP, a KISS and a HUG.

E.g. Loving is when you like someone so much you can't think of
anything else.
Loving is when you love someone and plan to get married and you
go out everywhere together.
Hating is when I don't like someone and I am steaming with hate.
Hating is when you have a row with someone and you want never
to speak to her again (you think).

A lap is where you can sit on and sleep in and lay in.
A lap is the top of your legs when you bend your legs.
A kiss is when you hold someone and put your lips on someone's lips
or cheek.
You kiss someone when you love them or when you are going to bed.
A hug is two people holding each other closely.
A hug is when a bear gets hold of you.

Drama and movement
Learn a number of dances — Dashing White Sergeant; Haste to the
Wedding, etc.

Mime three incidents; The young man takes out a young lady for the
first time, in his car — which has a number of mishaps: a Peeping Tom
who gets his deserts. The troubadour who sings at the wrong balcony.

Perform the stories of Daphnis and Chloe, and Cupid and Psyche.

Act the story of Helen of Troy.

Improvise the story of *The Frog Prince* or *Beauty and the Beast.*

Act the story of St. Valentine who was imprisoned in a Roman gaol,
and there restored the sight of a blind girl, the daughter of one of
his warders.

Tell the story of *Midsummer Night's Dream* as a play, mime or ballet.

Read *The Raggle Taggle Gipsies* and improvise a play from it.

Art
Prepare a collage picture of a bridal group.
Design and draw an engagement ring and a wedding ring.

Craft
Using card, tissue paper of various colours and doilies, prepare a
Valentine card.

With flowers make a buttonhole and a posy.

Make a mobile of the girls 'chasing' the boys — or is it the other
way round?

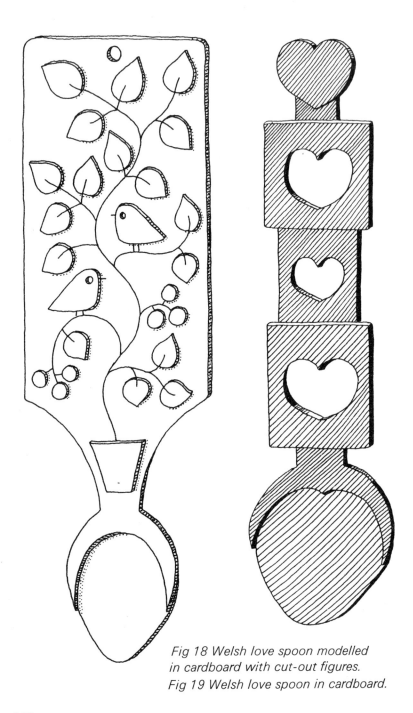

*Fig 18 Welsh love spoon modelled
in cardboard with cut-out figures.
Fig 19 Welsh love spoon in cardboard.*

Design a Welsh Love Spoon and make it in card or balsa wood.

Links with other festivals
Lupercalia – a Roman festival in honour of Pan.
A saint with local, national or international interest and affection –
St. Christopher, St. Nicholas, St. George.

an easter celebration

This is the most important festival in the Christian calendar, but in school its observance often takes second place to Christmas celebrations. One possible reason for this is the apparent dominance of the sadness of the Crucifixion. Yet without this, there would have been no suffering and no resurrection.

The class teacher responsible for the main work of this festival saw in it the culmination of a term's study of the Holy Land which had begun with the Feast of Epiphany. Influenced by the Oberammergau Passion Play, she took the principals from her own class, and used the remainder of the school as the crowd, who responded collectively and individually during the mounting crises of 'Holy Week'. Each day for seven days we watched and participated in the incidents which became our daily assembly theme. It was decided to portray the situation and activities of Good Friday in a different way and this was done by giving short news bulletins over the school radio. This was left switched on all day so that a sense of live reporting of the events could be achieved.

The Easter Christian Festival coincides with that point on the eternal rhythmic cycle associated with renewal and rebirth, and so manifestations of this are an important feature to include during these celebrations. By treating a festival in this way, vague impressions and ideas are brought into sharp focus.

INFORMATION AND INSPIRATION
Matthew 26 and 28
Mark 14 – 16
Luke 22 – 24
John 12 – 21

Books
Grebon, Arnoud: (Translated by James Kirkup)*True Mystery of the Passion.*
Heaton, V: *The Oberammergau Passion Play* (Hale).
Kendall, Joan: *Seven Days To Victory* (Blandford Press).
Passion Play Oberammergau 1960 (Benn).

Poetry
Bannerman, Frances: *An Upper Chamber*
Blake, William: *Holy Thursday*
Chesterton, G. K: *The Donkey*
Gallienne, Richard Le: *The Second Crucifixion*

Herbert, George: *Easter Song*
Hopkins, Gerard Manley: *Easter*
Masefield, John: *Good Friday*
Miller, May: *Calvary Way*
Muller, E: *Crucifixion*
Rodgers, W. R: *And when they had scourged Jesus*
Sansom, Clive: *The Donkey's Owner*
Vaughan, Henry: *Palm Sunday* and *Easter Hymn*

Music
Bach, J. S: *Magnificat*
　　　　Mass in B Minor
　　　　St. Matthew Passion
Handel, G: *The Messiah* (Part II)
Haydn, J: *Seven Last Words*
Schutz, Heinrich: *St. John Passion*
Stainer, John: *Crucifixion*
Wagner, R: *Good Friday Spell* from *Parsifal* (Act 3)
Mascagni, Pietro: The Easter Hymn from *Cavalleria Rusticana*

Hymns
All Glory Laud and Honour
Ride on Ride on in Majesty
There Is A Green Hill
When I Survey The Wondrous Cross
Jesus Christ Is Risen Today
The Strife Is O'er, the Battle done
The Head That Once Was Crowned With Thorns

See *Faith Folk and Festivity* (Galliard) for
Processional For Palm Sunday
When They Shouted Hosanna
Friday Morning
Come and Climb The Mountain
Good Friday
The Sun and The Hill
The Tree Springs To Life
Celebration Song
The Promise
I Will Be With You Always

Other aids
Films and filmstrip
The Passion Story (6 sections – EFVA)
The Passion (EFVA)
Life of Christ in Art, Gateway Films from Sound Services Ltd.
Inquest at Golgotha, Rank Films
The News on Good Friday, Rank Films
The First Easter, Rank Films
King of Kings, Rank Films

Record
Easter Sunday in Rome (Decca LXT 6251)

Pictures
Artists have illustrated the Crucifixion in many dramatic ways
throughout time:
Descent from the Cross, Rembrandt
Crucifixion, Gaugin
The Yellow Christ, Salvador Dali
The Last Supper, Stanley Spencer
And many of the great Italians such as Piero della Francesca.

Excursions
To a church to take part in an Easter service and see an Easter Garden.
On Good Friday to Dunstable Down, Bedfordshire, to see orange
rolling (symbolic of the rolling away of the stone from Christ's tomb?).
Pace-Egg play performed annually at Midgley, Yorkshire.
Easter Saturday for the Nutters' Dance at Bacup, Lancashire.
Easter Monday for egg rolling or pace egging at Preston, Lancs. (and
several other places).

CREATIVE ACTIVITIES
Writing
Write a story about the arrival of Jesus in Jerusalem on Palm Sunday.

A few days later write about the arrest and trial of Jesus, and explain
why you cheered him a few days before, and now you are ready to
see him crucified.

105

Write, in the form of a play, the court hearings and trial of Jesus.

You are a Roman soldier, guarding Jesus, and sympathetic to his cause. Write about the morning on the Hill of Calvary.

You were the Roman soldier on duty at the tomb. At your court martial explain how it was that the body of Jesus disappeared.

Prepare a book of poems about the events of Easter Week, and use these for choral presentation. Tuned percussion and other sound effects can be developed to accompany the poems or to act as punctuation.

Here are some examples written by some eleven-year-old children.

Hosanna, hosanna
The Messiah has come
Throw down your robes so that
He might be welcome

Out with the Romans
Out with The King
So HE might rule
He'll stop all the taxes
And stop all our payments
And then we'll be richer
And be full of gaiety

We'll be a happy city
Rich and so beautiful
That other cities
Will be jealous of our wonderful Messiah
Messiah of all.
Hosanna, hosanna, hosanna.   Michele

On a hot sunny day
Jesus did ride
Along the Streets of Jerusalem
Clip clop on an ass
With cloaks and palms
Thrown at his feet
He suddenly began to weep

And everyone thought it strange
And suddenly were afraid
They thought he would destroy them
Or the end of the world was coming.   Russell

BAZAAR WRECKAGE
There was a wreckage of
Stalls and money on the floor
And animals running and Jesus with a whip
With his hands he made a real mess
People running too, frightened and four
by four they ran to the door
Kicking, shoving, pushing and running
Terrified for their lives and pigeons
Squeaking and squawking and all that was
Left was up-turned tables and
Everybody peering through the door.   Michael

In the Gardens of Gethsemane
Went Jesus and his disciples *
He said 'Keep awake'
And pray for me

But lo — behold
They fell asleep
And Jesus said you could not keep awake

They said they were sorry
But they fell asleep again
And Jesus woke them up.

Again they fell asleep
And in their dream
There came a sound
'Help dear Father
Help me if you can'.

They woke again
And Jesus said
You can now go to sleep
For now it is too late

For Jesus could
Hear the sound
of tramping feet

The soldiers had come.   Pauline

Drama and movement
Using the Bible for reference, prepare the story of Easter as a series of
dramatic episodes which can be performed on several days or at one
performance.

Make a selection of readings and present the story, using slides bought
or borrowed from the National Gallery, Trafalgar Square, London, or the
filmstrips mentioned above, or slides taken of pictures prepared by the
children themselves. Play tape-recorded music to suit the mood of the
situation. Add other sound effects, e.g. donkey for Palm Sunday.
Listen to *The Easter Story* (E.M.I. record MFP 1215).

Learn *Lord of the Dance* (Galliard or on Galliard record GAL S4000).
Sing and dance this composition.

Link up the story of Christ's washing of the apostles' feet, and the
giving of Maundy money. Include in the dramatic episodes, James II,
who was the last monarch to wash the feet of his subjects; food and
clothing being given by Queen Elizabeth I to her subjects; the
distribution of specially-minted one-penny, two-penny, three-penny and
four-penny pieces in small white purses (to the value of one penny for
each year of the sovereign's age).

A Yeoman of the Guard carries the gifts of money on a gold tray.
Those taking part in the ceremony carry a posy of flowers and foliage as
a reminder of the time when herbs were used in the washing procedure.

Act the story of the Tuttimen of Hungerford, Berkshire, who each
Hocktide (two weeks after Easter) hold court. The 'justices' appoint
two men – the tutties – whose 'badge of office' is a large staff, on top of
which is a tutti or bouquet of flowers, adorned with ribbons and an
orange. These men are accompanied by the Orange scrambler whose hat
is made from cock's feathers. Every man pays his due of one penny;
each lady a kiss for which in return she receives an orange.

Perform the Mummers' Play associated with pace-egging. The hero is St George (as in traditional Christmas Mummers' Plays) who battles against many foes – the Black Prince of Paradine, Bold Slasher, Toss Pot, etc. and all the contestants are at various times treated by the Doctor. Toss Pot carries a basket of egg offerings. He wears a long ragged cloak, made up from pieces of cloth, and a straw tail. Others in the group wear bright tunics and helmets well decorated with ribbons and bells. Wooden swords are the weapons. Link with the pace-egging song mentioned elsewhere under this festival.

Listen to *A Man Dies* (EMI Record 33 SX 1609) and perform this as a dance drama.

Art

Paint a sequence of pictures for the hall showing scenes from Holy Week.

Use crayons to create 'stained glass' pictures of Christ's Crucifixion. Heavy black crayoning is required for the 'leads'. Brush cooking oil on the back of the completed window to render it translucent and mount over a window.

Paint directly onto the window the various symbols of Easter Week; the whip; nails; crown of thorns; the spear; chains; the cross; the tomb; etc.

Design a series of Easter cards which depict scenes from the Passion.

Design a number of cards which make use of the egg shape and its opening, to reveal a message.

Prepare a long frieze with chicks, rabbits, spring flowers, etc. Cut shapes from coloured paper and add to the picture.

Craft

Make an indoor Easter garden. On a large tray prepare a soil base, and there replant small flowers, or place them there in pots. Make up a tomb from papier mâché. Show the stone rolled away. Prepare figures, of Mary and the 'gardener' for example. With battery, bulb and short lengths of wire, light can be made to shine inside the deserted tomb.

Fig 20 Model of Easter garden.

Use lengths of balsa wood to make three crosses. In Plasticine or other modelling medium show the figures of Christ and the two robbers hanging from the crosses. Every child in the class can prepare bystanders, soldiers, priests, etc.

Prepare a number of clay tiles, about 6" x 6" and ½" (15 x 15 x 1 cm) thick. Use a modelling tool to incise in them the fourteen Stations of the Cross. When dry arrange to have the tiles biscuit-fired.

   I. Jesus is condemned to death.
  II. Jesus receives the cross.
 III. Jesus falls for the first time.
 IV. Jesus is met by his Mother.
  V. Simon of Cyrene helps to carry the cross.
 VI. Veronica wipes the face of Jesus.
VII. Jesus falls the second time.
VIII. Jesus speaks to the women of Jerusalem.
 IX. Jesus falls the third time.
  X. Jesus is stripped of his garment.
 XI. Jesus is nailed to the cross.
XII. Jesus dies on the cross.
XIII. Jesus is taken down from the cross.
XIV. Jesus is laid in the sepulchre.

Hot cross buns

These were formerly flat unleavened buns with very little shape. Now they are spicy and delicious and still have a cross on them. An interesting survey was carried out in Oxford in 1969 by a consumer association who found that the prices of buns varied from 4¼d. to 6d. and the weights from 4 oz. to 9 oz. Quantities of fruit, spice and candied peel varied tremendously and so incensed were some of the investigators that they asked professional advice on whether some traders were breaking the law by selling a hot cross bun cold! The project director summed the situation up by saying that unless buns were made properly, a child could grow up never knowing what a traditional bun tasted like. So here are the ingredients:

¾ lb. (300 g.) flour
½ oz. (12 g.) yeast
1 oz. (25 g.) sugar
¼ pint (125 ml.) and 2 tablespoonfuls of tepid water or milk
1 egg
1½ oz. (35 g.) currants and sultanas
1 oz. margarine
¼ teaspoonful of ground nutmeg
¼ teaspoonful of ground cinnamon
pinch of salt
– and here are the cooking instructions:

1. Place flour in a warm place and cream together the yeast with ¼ pint of tepid liquid sweetened with 1 teaspoonful of sugar.
2. Add salt, spices, dried fruit, sugar to the flour and mix well.
3. In a well, made in the flour, pour in a beaten egg and melted margarine, and then carefully add the cream yeast. This should become a sticky dough, with extra water where necessary.
4. Knead for 5 minutes, and then cover with a cloth and allow to rise in a warm place for about an hour.
5. Beat again and with floured hands divide up the dough into round portions, and place on a greased baking sheet allowing room for expansion.
6. Cut a cross in the top, and then allow another 15 minutes' 'proving' in a warm place.
7. Baking in a hot oven, 450° F (230° C) should be for 20 minutes.

Pace eggs (Paschal = Passion = Easter).

Eggs are hardboiled after being wrapped with onion skins and other natural materials, so that they become coloured. Names and patterns can be inscribed with a candle before wrapping and boiling, so that the waxed area resists the dye.

Eggs can be rolled down the side of a steep hill to see which remain intact or can be used to jab another, turn by turn to see which one will remain unbroken.

Learn the *Pace Egging Song* (recorded on Topic record 12T 136 and EMI record SZL P 2103).

Eggs can be decorated in other ways. Felt pens can be used for drawing designs and ribbons, wool, straw, spaghetti, macaroni, etc. can be stuck on with Copydex. Small sections of papier mâché egg boxes can be cut to act as a stand or cup for the decorated egg.

Fig 21 Easter egg designs.

Eggs that are fresh can be blown, by piercing a small hole at one end (through which one blows) and a large hole at the other. Such shells can be used to make up figures and shapes, e.g. serpents, birds with feather embellishment.

Egg dyeing and pattern work is another craft which can be introduced at this time. Dyes can be obtained from Schmidt's, 41 Charlotte Street, London W.1, and Schliephak and Stevenson Ltd., 42 Charlotte Street, London, W.1.

Dip the hardboiled egg into a light dye and allow it to dry. With a pinhead heated in a candle flame, place spots of molten beeswax on the egg surface in a pattern. Arrange elastic bands over the egg to create areas for the hot wax application. Now immerse the egg into a darker dye (for half an hour) and allow to dry. With care hold egg over a gas flame and when the wax melts, rub it away to reveal the pattern of the lighter dye below. The egg can also be patterned by arranging elastic bands of various thicknesses around the surface of the egg after the first dipping and then immersing again to provide a contrasting colour. (See also *Painted Easter Eggs,* Leisure Craft Series – Burns and Oates.)

Design an Easter bonnet
Use old hats as a basis for development and then staple card to existing brims and cover with silks and satins – and tissue paper. See diagram overleaf. Remember a ribbon to hold the hat on, and a matching parasol. Hold a parade, with background music *In her Easter bonnet, With all the flowers upon it.*

Young children will enjoy making nests of cut paper, sitting a cardboard cut-out hen inside, and surrounding it with bought confectionery eggs.

Prepare and cook a Simnel cake
(Considered suitable for Easter Sunday as well as Mothering Sunday.)
Ingredients:
8 oz. (225 g.) mixed fruit and chopped peel.
4 oz. (115 g.) sugar
4 oz. (115 g.) fat
2 eggs
Grated rinds of half a lemon and half an orange
A little milk

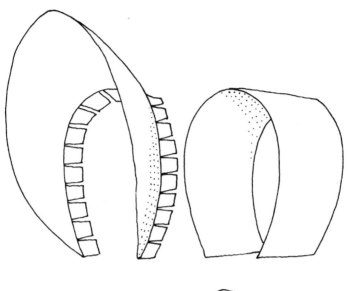

Fig 22 Easter bonnet.

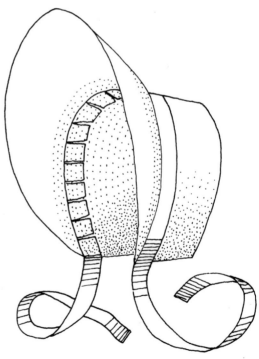

8 oz. (225 g.) flour
1 level tsp. baking powder
8 oz. (225 g.) almond paste
Pinch of salt
$\frac{1}{4}$ tsp.ginger, cinnamon and nutmeg

Method:
1. Grease and line a cake tin.
2. Cream the fat and sugar and add beaten eggs.
3. Add the orange and lemon rind and sieve into mixture the flour, salt, spices and baking powder. Add milk until the consistency is soft.
4. Fold in the fruit and then divide into two. Place half into the tin and smooth down.
5. Cover with a layer of almond paste, and top with the rest of the mixture.
6. Cook in a moderate oven, 325° F (165° C) for about 3 hours.
7. When cold decorate with another layer of almond paste and add small chocolate eggs and woolly chicks.

Take these lines of Robert Herrick and make an arrangement of box leaves.

Down with the Rosemary and Baies
Down with the Mistletoe,
Instead of holly, now uprise
The greener Box for show.
The holly hithertoe did sway;
Let box now domineer,
Until the dancing Easter Day
Or Easter Eve appear.

Links with other festivals
Spring, Christmas.

A Celebration of May

This, of all the festive occasions of the year, is essentially an outdoor affair. The sad fact of course is that the weather for the summer term cannot be guaranteed. The cynics and pessimists who describe the English summer as being 'one fine day followed by a thunderstorm' or the period between July 31st and August 1st' are exaggerating a little. Nevertheless in planning an outdoor festival it is advisable to be prepared for the worst. By arranging for an afternoon early in the week,

Plate 5 Tripping it on the green.
(*Keystone Press Agency Ltd*)

a postponement to the Wednesday or Thursday is feasible. If the school hall is sufficiently large then this could be got ready — just in case.

Certainly many of the items to be included within a programme can be practised indoors. One is always trying to achieve a gay spontaneity in all such occasions as this; nevertheless dances and other activities need to be learnt. The important thing is to avoid too many weeks of gruelling rehearsal but to rely on a number of stalwarts to carry the programme through and not to fly into a rage if someone drops a ribbon during an intricate part of the maypole dance.

In a memorial programme for Sir Malcolm Sargent, his son recalled a situation as a child, when he was invited to hand around the drinks to some distinguished visitors, and he tripped over and upset the tray — and his father. Afterwards, Sir Malcolm asked his son what he had tripped over, and he replied 'You, father'. I think that many of our children, in performance, are so anxious not to make a mistake because of us, that their performances are inhibited and things go wrong.

We tried an interesting experiment with our May Celebration by organising it as part of a fair. In our indoor festival we expect everyone to be attentive, and by arranging a programme with variety and pace we hope that this attention will be voluntary, rather than imposed. For the great outdoors, however, we wanted to create something like the colourful bedlam of Derby Day. But just as on that occasion there is what is described as the serious business of racing horses, so in our celebration there were regular parts of the afternoon given over to the organised programme. Sideshows were set up and operated throughout the afternoon and stalls with drinks, cakes and traditional sweets were open for business. These were all run by the children, who also carried around home-made sweets and fruit, lavender bags, pomanders, handkerchiefs and ribbons, crying their wares.

There was a Pie Poudre Court set up, to try to punish those who in some way offended during the proceedings. A period of time in the stocks, to be pelted with wet sponges, was the fate of any miscreant. (In fact this 'punishment' was so enjoyed by many of the children that the law was abused on several occasions.)

A town crier, a boy with a tremendous voice, which I envied, announced each part of the programme, and people — parents and

Plate 6 The May Queen and the Green King.
(*Pace Ltd*)

children — gathered around the arena. This was not well enough
cordoned off, and it became smaller and smaller as the day wore on!
By the use of two long extension leads, power was brought out onto
our small grass area, and sufficient amplification was obtained from the
portable gramophone player. Events of the day are included in the
creative activities which follow.

One of the great events of South London at this time of year is the
Festival of Singing Games at Redriff School, Rotherhithe. About 1960,
the headmistress, Mrs. Mary Wilson, began her outdoor festival with her
younger children. With tremendous energy and enthusiasm, her venture
has grown, and ten years later, she was inviting 2,300 children to a
three-day gathering. Her own children acted as leaders and helped to
organise children from many different schools who had learnt their

dances at their home base. Domestic arrangements for toilets, supply of drinks, provision of bases for each visiting group for picnics, indoor plans in case of bad weather etc., were all splendidly organised. A control centre was set up in a classroom with several microphones and an amplifier, and the broadcasts were relayed to several points in the playing field where there were loudspeakers. This equipment is loaned by the local authority and used imaginatively by Mrs. Wilson. From the window of the classroom she can see almost the whole area and so she is able to direct the whole operation with military precision. Two choirs are used in the studio, singing alternate items to boost the efforts of the dancers outside. The school have now recorded a large selection of their singing games under the Topic label, IMP-A 101, and there is an accompanying book of words, music and instructions for such traditional games as Sally Go Round The Moon, Round and Round The Village, The Jolly Miller, Dusky Bluebells, Green Gravel, The Big Ship and Oranges and Lemons. (*The Festival Book of Singing Games* by Mary Wilson and Jennifer Gallagher.)

INFORMATION AND INSPIRATION

The second verse of the *Furry Song* (from Helston in Cornwall) runs so —
And we were up as soon as any Day O
And For To fetch the Summer home
For Summer is a-come O
And Winter is a go O
With Ha-lan-tow
Jolly Rumble O.

It is sung at the May Festival and reminds everyone that this is a celebration for the arrival of summer. This is the morning when maidens would rise early to wash in the dew. The young men would also be up — as early — to fetch the summer home, in the shape of a great tree which they could set up as a maypole. This carrying of the tree spirit into the village, would ensure fruitfulness for the village and all who lived in it. The Puritans, however, put an end to this festival, as they did to so many features of life which had such elements of happiness and joyful abandon.

John Ruskin revived the celebration at Whitelands College in Putney, and the spread of the idea throughout primary schools in Britain, with dancing and the election of a May Queen, stems from that time and place.

120

It is interesting to note the way in which this day has been chosen by the workers of Eastern and Western Europe, with large union rallies and parades in Britain and displays of military might by the Communist nations. But their celebrations are rather serious and fortunately over in a day – we have thirty-one days from which to choose – if holidays or weekends intrude upon the first of the month.

Books and publications
MacMahon, D.: *May Festival* (a book from E.F.D.S.S., Cecil Sharp House, 2 Regents Road, London, N.W.1.)
May Day and its Traditions (leaflet from E.F.D.S.S.)

Poetry
Bennett, Sterndale: *May Queen Pastoral.*
Herrick, Robert: *Corinna's going a-Maying.*
Morley, Thomas: *Now Is The Month of Maying.*
Reeves, James: *May Day.*
Rosetti, C.: *Summer.*
Shakespeare, W.: *Where The Bee Sucks.*

Music
The Floral Dance
Salford Maypole Song (Poetry and Song – Macmillan)
Trotting To The Fair
Widdecombe Fair
Strawberry Fair
Scarborough Fair
Brigg Fair (Delius)
Mock Morris and *Shepherd's Hey* (Percy Grainger arrangements).

Excursions
Visit a nearby village celebration.

Exchange invitations with other schools celebrating May Day.

Schools in the neighbourhood of the following places, or on school journey to the area may like to witness and join in May festivities there.

Oxford, Magdalen College Tower: Singing of the Latin hymn *Te Deum Patrem Colimus* at 6 a.m. Morris dancing in the High Street.
Early morning swim in River Cherwell (in place of the bathing in dew).

A record, E 7610, *May Morning at Magdalen College, Oxford,* can be purchased through Discourses Ltd., 10A High Street, Tonbridge.

Knutsford, Cheshire: Parade of traditional figures including Jack-in-the-green, Robin Hood. Crowning of May Queen. Maypole dancing.

Padstow, Cornwall: To commemorate the occasion in 1346, when the men of Padstow were away at the siege of Calais, and a French privateer approached the Cornish port. A grotesque hobby horse was taken up to Stepper Point high above the harbour to frighten away the invaders.

Minehead, Somerset: On the eve of May Day, six fishermen parade through the town one dressed up as a be-ribboned hobby horse. The animal swishes its tail at anyone who scorns the collecting box.

Gawthorpe: May Feast at Ossett in Yorkshire. Long procession with decorated horses and carriages. May Queen. Maypole dancing.

Helston, Cornwall (May 8th): Day-long dancing in and out of houses by scores of couples dressed for a garden party.

Ickwell, Bedfordshire (last Saturday in May): Singing of Night Song and Day Song. Distribution of Maybushes to houses where there is a young maiden inside. Dancing around a very tall maypole. Lord and 'Lady' (another man dressed in female garments) and their black-faced counterparts – The Moggies – go around collecting tributes of beer, money or food.

Hungerford, Berkshire (May eve): Hocktide Court with twelve members or Feoffes deal with disputes concerning property and common rights. Two tutti-men or bailiffs are appointed to collect tolls and kisses. The toll is paid by the men, the caress by the ladies, who receive fruit from the Orange Scrambler.

Whalton, Northumberland: Midsummer or Bale Fire. A celebratory bonfire in honour of the sun and in the hope of good harvests in the ensuing weeks.

Royal Hospital, Chelsea (Founder's Day, May 29th): Statue of Charles II smothered in oak leaves. Pensioners wear a sprig of oak leaves on this Oak Apple Day, recalling the dramatic escape of the King, who is purported to have hid in an oak tree at Boscobel, following his rout at the Battle of Worcester in September 1651.

CREATIVE ACTIVITIES
Write a story about being lost in a fairground.

Describe in an illustrated account, a great May Day parade.

Write a poem about a May Queen and her election.

Drama and movement
Choose a Miracle Play, e.g. *The Fall of Lucifer* and perform it on a wagon (borrowed from local Parks Department).

Arrange a Pie Poudre Court, after researching into the type of offence which might have been committed in those days, and determine suitable punishments.

Perform the story of Petrouchka (with Stravinsky's music).

Learn Maypole and other country dances.

Invent a new dance and prefix it with the name of the school.

The following items will be useful:
Maypole Dances, W. Shaw (from E.F.D.S.S.)
Maypole Dances (Curwen & Co.)
Folk Dancing, R. Nettell (Arco)
English Folk Dancing of Today and Yesterday, Douglas Kennedy (Bell)
Morris and Sword Dances of England (ED 102, E.D.F.S.S.)
Country Dances for a May Festival, E7P317, and a book of instructions, W. Paxton Ltd.

Parade of May queens and attendants. Parade of Green Kings.
Election and coronation.

Art
Produce a large frieze showing a May Fair and invite everyone in the school to add a figure or item.

Make up a collage picture of a team of Morris Dancers.

Paint a picture of a May Queen surrounded by her attendants.

In Minsterley in Shropshire, the Betley Window shows the traditional characters joining in games around the maypole. Using crayons, make up a 'stained glass' window of a similar scene. Use black crayon for the 'leading' or strips of black tape. Cover back of picture with cooking oil to make it translucent and hang against the window.

Craft

With branches of flowering hawthorn decorate the doors of the school on May day.

Using hawthorn and other greenery, coloured paper, etc. prepare a throne and stage for the May Queen.

Make up costume for a team of morris dancers, including 'garters' of bells purchased from a large toy shop.

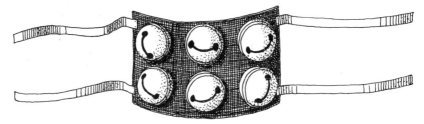

Fig 23 Bell garters for morris dancers.

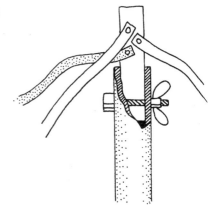

Fig 24 Making a maypole using a block of wood with ribbons attached, bolted into the top of a netball post.

Adapt a netball post to make a maypole, if this does not exist in the school. Alternatively ask a local park keeper or forester whether a group of boys might come and receive a tree with all the branches brashed off. Decorate with ribbons, hoops draped with greenery, posies of flowers and a crown. A barrel or dustbin will be needed to hold the pole which should be packed around with sand and gravel.

Make the Sailor's Horse from Minehead. It is seven or eight feet long, and two pliable lengths of wood this length are required. They should be tied together at each end and then braced apart by two short lengths of wood, between which the wearer will stand. Material should be cut and fixed to the top and from this, lengths of gaily coloured nylon and cotton should be sewn. A skirt of brightly coloured material has to be sewn around the frame. A tall conical mask is made up and fixed in position above the struts. A pair of tapes is also fixed to these for use as braces.

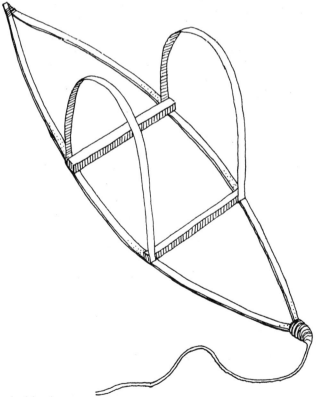

Fig 25 Frame for hobby horse.

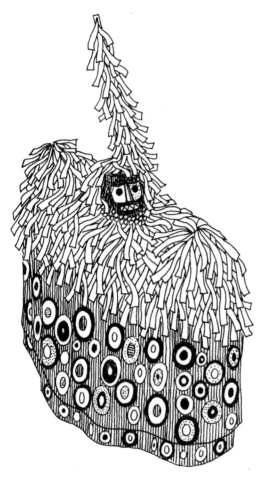

Fig 26 The completed hobby horse – the Sailor's Horse from Minehead.

Make up a Padstow hobby horse. For this a large hoop is needed, and this can be made up by using handle cane. Black shiny material has to be cut to cover this hoop and provide a skirt. Once again a large conical headpiece and mask is cut to fit over the space left in the top for the head and shoulders of the wearer.

Make up Tutti-poles or decorated sticks. Any length of wood will do and flowers and foliage are used to embellish these. Smaller strips of wood can be nailed to one end to provide a support for the material, and wire rings can be made up to build up the shapes required. Small pieces of chicken wire are useful too. The smallest mesh should be used and the wire squashed into the shape required — a ball, crown etc.

Dolls can be dressed as May queens and paraded in prams which have been decorated with foliage from the hawthorn tree.

Links with other festivals
Midsummer Festival; Country Fayre; an Elizabethan Celebration.

A Festival of Flowers

Great cathedrals and tiny churches now make a regular feature of Flower Festivals, and such places seem admirably suited to these displays. There is an enthusiastic interest in town and country evening classes, clubs and institutes for lessons and practice in the art of flower arrangement. We thought we would have a Flower Festival instead of the usual Harvest Festival, and the year we chose to do this, our 'Mother' church of Boxgrove in Sussex were taking their turn in Sussex by adorning their beautiful Priory which gives our school its name.

We were able to visit the display and learn much from it. Most such flower festivals decide to adopt a theme and illustrate it with flowers and foliage. Our choice was the History of the School – brief as it was. We decided upon early autumn, but in fact celebrations could equally well go on during the spring and summer, and even the winter, providing one had made adeqaute preparations and were willing to go above the 50 pence per class which we allowed to supplement gifts with special flowers because of their shape, colour or size.

Where a school decides to illustrate a number of different aspects e.g. its observances of religious festivals such as Easter, Harvest and Christmas; its connections with the town or city where it is; some distinguished person or event in history; a local industry or raw materials; a sporting personality or team, etc., it is a good idea to produce a simple guide sheet. A brief explanation of each exhibit or group will assist the viewer in coming to the intended conclusion. The preparation of the explanatory notes provides a good opportunity for writing where brevity and precision are vital.

INFORMATION AND INSPIRATION
Books
This is a selection of the very many, beautifully illustrated books available. Most of the pioneers are featured.

Baillie, John: *Meditation in Flowers* (Clarius Publications).
Clements, Julia: *A.B.C. of Flower Arrangements* (Pearson).
　　　　　　The Gift Book of Flower Arranging (Newnes).

129

Coe, Stella: *The Art of Japanese Flower Arrangement* (Jenkins).
Emberton, Sybil: *Garden Foliage for the Flower Arranger* (Faber and Faber).
Fleming, Joy: *Taste and Talent With Flowers* (Harrap).

MacQueen, Sheila: *Flower Decoration in Churches* (Faber and Faber).
Nichols, Beverley: *The Art of Flower Arrangement* (Collins).
Rogers, Joyce: *Flower Arranging All The Year Round* (Paul Hamlyn).
Smith, George: *Flower Arrangements and Their Settings* (Studio Vista).

Soutar, Merelle: *The Driftwood Flower Arrangement Book* (Arlington).
Spry, Constance: *Favourite Flowers* and
    Flower Decoration (Dent).

Stevenson, Violet: *Amateur Gardening Picture Book of Flower Arrangements* (Collingridge).

The Pulbrook and Gould Book of Flower Arrangement (Cresset).

Poetry
Blake, William: *Wild Flowers Song*
Clare, John: *To A Primrose*
Herrick, Robert: *To Daffodils*
Reeves, James: *Beech Leaves*
Shakespeare, W.: *Where the Bee sucks*
Webb, Mary: *The Secret Joy, The Snowdrop, The Wild Rose, Little Things*
Wordsworth, William: *I wandered lonely as a cloud*

Music
Flower song from *Carmen* by Bizet
The Flowers That Bloom in the Spring from *The Mikado* by Gilbert and Sullivan
Where Have All The Flowers Gone (Seegar)
Flowers of the Valley (S. Baring Gould's and Cecil Sharp's collection of English Folk Songs)
The Evening Primrose
Ballad of Green Broom (Benjamin Britten)
The Cornish Floral Dance
Flowers of the Forest

Film
The Language of Flowers (Rank)

Excursions
Visit flower displays in churches, town halls, agricultural shows, etc.
Visit garden nurseries and parks.
Visit Chelsea Flower Show, and provincial equivalents.
Visit Wisley Gardens, Kew Gardens, Sheffield Park Gardens, Sussex, etc.
National Gardens Scheme lists those grounds which are open during
various weekends of the year, in aid of various charities.
Visit a municipal or private garden where flowers are grown to
illustrate a particular theme, e.g. important anniversaries, voluntary
organisation badge, etc; or where there is a special feature e.g. the
Floral Clock in Princes Street, Edinburgh.
Plan an excursion to the Floral Hall, Covent Garden.
Travel one of the Kent blossom routes in early Summer.
Visit the bulb fields of Lincolnshire in spring time.
Visit the Channel Islands to witness the Battle of the Flowers.
Visit Tissington (Derbyshire) on Ascension Day to see the Ceremony
of the Blessing of the Wells and see the floral mosaics. (Also in other
villages in Derbyshire in June and July – details from Information
Bureau, Buxton, Derbyshire.)

CREATIVE WORK
Writing
Write a poem in praise of a sunflower or a snowdrop.
Use a gardening book to collect together the names of as many flowers
as possible. Arrange these in an order for rhythmic speaking, e.g.
Daffodil and daisy; Delphinium and dahlia;
Dandelion and dodder; Dogwood and dew berry, etc.
Write a story of a lady and her window box.
Write a story for assembly in which a bunch of flowers was passed
from hand to hand, until it arrived back at the home of the original giver.
Write a story of your early morning visit to Covent Garden to deliver
your flowers.

Drama and movement
Develop a story in which a 'saboteur' was attempting to spoil the efforts
of the growers of prize dahlias – and how he got his just deserts.

Produce a ballet story of the growth of plants from seed to maturity, with pollination by the wind and bees and the final scattering of seed. Experiment with excerpts of music, e.g.
Quick light movements: Dance of the Ethiopians from *Sylvia* (Delibes).
Slow and light movements: Waltz from *Coppelia* (Delibes).
Quick: Flight of the bumble bee from *Tsar Sultan* by Rimsky-Korsakov.
Slow and strong alternating with quick and strong: Jupiter from *Planets* by Holst.
Consult the Bible — Leviticus 23 — where God tells Moses that he was to keep a feast. Enact this story, with foliage and flowers.
Perform the opening sequence of *Pygmalion* (or *My Fair Lady*) when Professor Higgins first meets Eliza Doolittle.

Art

Try finger painting of flowers, with specimens for inspiration.
Crayon a picture of Puck anointing the eyes of the sleeping Titania with a flower.
Make a school frieze with every child invited to add a flower in any medium.
Take a piece of stout card or hardboard and cover it with thick layers of different-coloured crayons. To a small quantity of dark powder colour, add four or five times the quantity of washing-up liquid. When dry, use any sharp tool to cut away the top layer to reveal colours below. Incise petal forms to make up a floral picture.
Cut the shape of a flower head on a sliced potato or piece of lino and print a flower picture.
Create a flower calendar, in which flowers in bloom each month are shown. (Send for Flower Chart (and other useful leaflets) from Flowers and Plants Council, Agriculture House, Knightsbridge, London, S.W.1.).
Make up a collage picture of a flower seller in Piccadilly. Select materials — paper or cloth — and stick with Copydex to a heavy card background.

Craft

From early spring to autumn make collections of wild flowers.
Carefully arrange these between sheets of newspaper and apply pressure for a few days (with books, weights, etc.) and then stick to paper or card with gum. Arrangements can be made under glass tops of tables, behind finger panels on doors or in books and chosen in particular ways, by colour, by size, or by habitat.

Make a miniature garden. In a metal or otherwise waterproof tray, filled with soil or sand, arrange flowers, foliage, and objects to suggest a small garden.

Prepare flowers in special arrangements, e.g. a gentleman's buttonhole, a wedding bouquet, in an egg-cup, using only three blooms.

Decorate a go-cart or pram with flowers, using florist's wire to attach the stems securely. Alternatively, a layer of fine mesh chicken wire can be fastened over the 'vehicle' and flowers fixed in this way.

In autumn, plant daffodil, narcissus and tulip bulbs in a bowl or pot of fibre. The pot should be placed in a dry, cool cupboard for about ten weeks, ensuring that the fibre is moist. After this time, it should be taken out into a cool, light room. The blooms should be ready just before Easter and available for a Spring Flower display.

Purchase seed for early summer planting, e.g. Nasturtium. Tendrils, leaves and flowers can be persuaded to grow on small canes, etc., arranged in the container.

Collect seedpods, pods, and flowers in July and August for drying to use in winter displays, e.g. irises, honesty, grasses.

Hang these upside down in cool dark cupboards to ensure good drying and avoid bleaching or mildewing. Foilage — beech and oak for instance, can be preserved. Collect while green, and put their stems in a mixture of one part of glycerine to two parts of warm water, for two weeks. Use these in late autumn or at Christmas in a floral display.

Make an arrangement of flowers
Here are some suggestions for those who are attempting this craft for the first time.
Choose the flowers with their purpose kept in mind, i.e. selected for their suitability to illustrate a theme, contrast, etc.

Select flowers not yet developed into their full beauty, i.e. roses should be closed and buddy, daffodils firm, only a few of the gladioli flowers open.

Remember that some flowers will last longer than others, e.g. the flowers of the end of the year last longer than those of spring and summer. Flowers available all the year round last longer than those with a short season. (Second bloom roses don't last as long as first.)

Flowers need cool conditions with plenty of fresh air.

Always snip an inch or so off the stems before putting in water; in the case of woody stems, hammer the lowest two inches; always remove leaves on stems which would lie below the water line; keep a good supply of cool, clean water available.

Collect as many types of container as possible, so that the right size, shapes and colour can be selected.
Arrange to have a supply of wide-gauge chicken wire, crumpled up, to set in the bottom of a container to take the stems of flowers, or purchase a pack of oasis from the florists for this purpose.
Decide upon your basic shape for the display, think about the colours of the flowers you wish to have, their size and number.

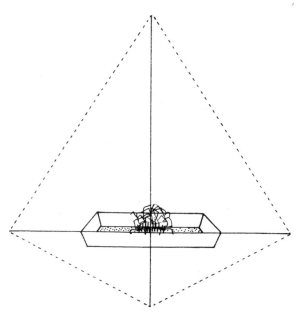

Fig 27 Plan for flower arrangement. Height about one and a half times width of dish. Side widths about two-thirds of height. Depth about a third of the height.

134

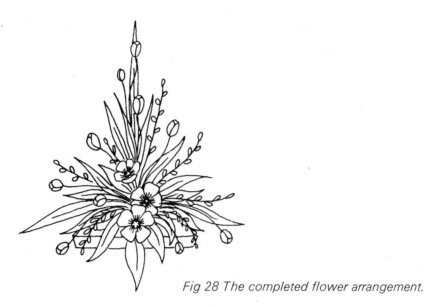

Fig 28 The completed flower arrangement.

In the case of a classic arrangement in triangular form, select a tall flower, approximately one and a half times the height of the container (or the breadth in the case of a low flat vessel). Add flowers to fill out the central line, with stems getting shorter and shorter until the lowest is just over the brim.

Now set other flowers in place, at an angle, so that they all meet at a central place just below the central stem. Ensure that some flowers are at the rim of the container. Heavier blooms and deeper colours should be used low down and near the centre of the display.

To make an asymmetrical design, begin by putting some tall stems on the left of the display, and others almost horizontally off to the right. Add tall and heavier flowers to the vertical line when the shape has been decided upon, and then longer slender stems and flowers to the right, so that they will droop below the line.

Practise making arrangements often.

When a theme has been adopted, then a real connection with this should be aimed for, rather than an absolute concentration upon getting a lovely design. Originality and ingenuity are the qualities which are looked for – there is very little creativity in copying.

After such a festival as this, the children can be invited, at various other regular intervals throughout the year, to produce arrangements for the hall, library, main foyer, etc.

Prepare a well-dressing picture. On a wooden frame (the bigger the better) spread a layer of clay — which must be kept moist. Select a biblical text and using petals, complete flowers, moss, greenery, seeds, etc., illustrate the chosen theme. (See *The Beauty and Mystery of Well-Dressing*, Creighton Porteous (Pilgrim Press, Derby).)

Urban schools, or those with children living in flats, can build window boxes of wood, and plant these with seeds.

Using a copy of *Indoor Gardening* (Wills and Hepworth) develop ideas for growing plants in school.

Links with other festivals
Trees; Animals.

Safely gathered in—
A Festival of
the Earth

One's experiences, especially in childhood, can significantly affect one's view of the present, and in late summer and autumn if I am in the countryside watching the great, red, combine harvester swallowing up vast fields of wheat, I think back nostalgically to the 'old days'. Then, and I hope this does not date me too much, as boys we would join the men in the fields at 7.30 a.m. (where they had been for a couple of hours already). We would help to drive the horses pulling those quaint machines – the reaper binders. Then we had to stand or shock up the sheaves which had been untidily dropped behind the Heath Robinson machines. Then came the job of carting the harvest to the stack yard, and the building of the stack, all hard, dusty but satisfying work. The next joy was to watch the peripatetic threshing machine remove the grain from the stalk and you knew it was all safely gathered in.

The Harvest Festival and supper was a real event in the countryside. It was a very sincere form of thanksgiving – one of the oldest ceremonies of man – much older than Christianity, and so deeply ingrained in our being that its celebration is almost as eagerly awaited as the Christmas Festival. This is certainly true of schools when in late September and early October, children can be seen taking their offerings of vegetables (and groceries) to church and school for a special service.

Last year we invited our children to write down their thoughts about Harvest Festivals. Here is a selection of their comments.

'Harvest is in the month of October. We have Harvest Festival to thank God for food. We bring some kind of fruit.'

'You give it to the old people. The old people are very thankful for the fruit and sometimes write a thank-you letter.'

'I think harvest is a good idea. At harvest time we give food to the old people and have a special play. At harvest time, the farmers collect all their crops. It is also a thanksgiving to God for food. In school we take food and flowers to give to people less fortunate than us.'

'A harvest festival is a time when we sell things and sing songs and the mums and dads come.'
'Giving things makes people happy.'

'Our parents come and we all say thank you to them and they are happy to know that you think they are good too.'

But occasionally one gets some straight-from-the-shoulder comment, which would never have been written in the time of the reaper-binder. We never complained or dissented then — perhaps we didn't know we could!

'I don't know why we need harvest festivals. I think they have come down to us as a celebration — but I don't know why they have it.'

'A harvest festival is a teacher's and headmaster's festival.' Hmmmm!

It is a good idea to give a different look to the celebration, if possible every year, while still retaining certain familiar elements. One might invite a speaker from a church or the local community to give a short address. A colleague in another school might be prepared to do this in return for a similar service to his school on another occasion.

This is a very colourful time of the year, and efforts should be made to make the hall and school look suitably attractive.

Children enjoy bringing along their gifts to school, and even here there is room for a variation. Local names can be collected of the old, lonely and sick who might like to receive a parcel taken round by the children; a local organisation who run a welfare and recreational service will appreciate such gifts, especially if they are packeted or tinned groceries; the local old people's home or a hospital would make use of such offerings; the goods can be sold and the proceeds given to an organisation, local, national or international, who concern themselves with the needs of the hungry and homeless (see Festival of Good Neighbours).

It is interesting to see reference to the pioneering work of the Rev. R. S. Hawker who is purported to have held the first harvest festival on October 1st, 1843, and that in 1862 a Convocation of Canterbury issued a form of service.

INFORMATION AND INSPIRATION
Books
Duddington, C. L: *Useful Plants* (McGraw Hill)

Edwards, D. J: *Growing Food* (Rupert Hart Davis).
Elwell, F: *Science and the Farmer* (Bell).
Huggett, Frank: *Farming* (Black).
Hvass, E: *Plants that Feed Us* (Blandford).
Ladyman, P: *About Farm Machines* (Brockhampton).
Redmayne, Paul: *Britain's Food* (John Murray).

Poetry
Betjeman, John: *Diary of a Church Mouse*
Davies, W. H: *Rich Days*
Drinkwater, J: *Moonlit Apples*
Heaney, Seamus: *Blackberry Picking*
Hood, Thomas: *Ruth*
Hopkins, Gerard Manley: *Hurrahing in Harvest*
Keats, J: *Autumn*
Kirkup, James: *The Lonely Scarecrow*
Lee, Laurie: *Apples*
Mullineaux, Peter: *Harvest Festival*
Pasternak, L: *Haystacks*
Sackville-West, V: *Harvest* (from 'The Land')
Thomas, Edward: *Haymakers*
Wordsworth, W: *The Solitary Reaper*

Music
Beethoven, L: *Symphony No. 6* (Pastoral – 3rd movement).
Vivaldi: *The Four Seasons* (Autumn).
Harvest Thanksgiving – a cantata by Malcolm Williamson recorded on Tower record, CLM206 (from Joseph Weinberger Ltd., 33 Crawford Court, London, W.1).
The Fruit of the tree (Harvest Carol) (Galliard Ltd. – also in
    Sing Round the Year – Bodley Head).
Hoe Down (from *Seven Brides for Seven Brothers*).
Music for Barn Dances (see May Festival).

Songs
John Barleycorn
Your hay it is moved (from *King Arthur* by Dryden and Purcell).
Farmer, Farmer sow your seed
Green corn
One man went to mow

Oats and beans and barley grow
Miller of Dee
Kum Bah Ya (with adaptation of verses to suit the particular needs of
 the occasion).

Excursions

To a church harvest festival (preferably in the country and giving
prior warning to the vicar).
Visit to a farm at harvest time if the farmer will permit an intrusion at
this time.
A museum where agriculture is featured, e.g. Science Museum, South
Kensington; Castle Museum, York; Folk Museum, Gloucester.
Visit to a mill or a bakery.
To the countryside to gather a harvest from the hedgerow.

Films

Village in the wheatfields (Greenpark Prod. and NCVAE).
Grain Harvest — Scotland 1936 (Rank Films).

CREATIVE ACTIVITIES
Writing

The weather is bad; the harvest must be gathered before morning.
Write about the gathering of the crops by night.

Write a newspaper report of a village harvest festival celebration.
Write a poem about the combine harvester at work in the fields.
Create a pattern of sound words in your poem. Set this to music.
Write a song about the Loaves and the Fishes (Matthew 15, Mark 6,
 Luke 9).
Compose prayers to accompany Gifts from the Harvest of the Field,
 Orchard, Garden, Hedgerow, Tree, etc.
Psalm 65 is most appropriate for choral speech or singing. Write a
Harvest Psalm after discussing and using the biblical poem.

Drama and movement

Act the story of The Sower (Matthew 13.3, Mark 4.3; Luke 8.5).
Act the story of Ruth.
Tell the story of Joseph as a dance-drama (Music — *Joseph and The
 Amazing Technicoloured Dream Coat* — Novello. Recorded on
 Decca, SKL 4973).

Create a dance based on the Abbots Bromley Horn Dance (held early in September). Six dancers carry horned deer heads; Robin Hood, Maid Marian, a Fool and an Archer join in to the music of concertina and triangle.

Make a movement play of the story of Persephone. (E.M.I. record 7 E.G. 8976.)

Tell the story of Hiawatha's fight with Mondamin using Longfellow's words. Mime the action.

Produce a Ballet of the Seeds — contrast popping seeds, flying seeds, whirling seeds, and swaying seeds. Add sound effects to music.

Mime the story of the gathering of the harvest, processing of the flour and conversion into boxed cereals. Select music, or use word patterns and machine noises.

Act out the story of a reaping race between three men, supported by their wives. (See the short story *The Reaping Race* by Liam O'Flaherty.)

Perform the story of the Little Red Hen who was refused help to plant, care for, harvest and transport her crop — and managed to eat her bread all by herself too.

Organise a Barn Dance to be held as part of the secular celebrations. Team of dancers learn different dances, and teach the others.

Art

Make up a large group picture showing the whole seasonal process of preparation, sowing, augmentation and harvest.

Make a picture of the harvesters at work, contrasting the modern methods with the older ways of doing the job.

Paint card black and cut out silhouette shapes of beams, implements, farmyard animals to decorate the hall for a barn dance (add bales of hay, sheaves of corn — often available from churches after their own celebrations, if one is in an urban school).

Prepare an autumn frieze with birds and animals of the hedgerow and field. Prepare a tape recording, taking from records appropriate sound effects, (see appendix I Sounds for Celebrations), or make recordings using portable machines on an excursion.

A short length of tape, so prepared can be made up into a loop, and played continuously. (See appendix.)

142

Craft

Make up a model farm, using scrap materials for fields, crops, buildings, etc. Various scale models of commercial farm vehicles and figures can be added to the model.

Gather samples of as many grain and other crops and arrange in a display with country of origin on map linked with coloured threads. Use tables to make into fruit and vegetable carts. Laths strapped to the table legs can support coloured awnings of paper or other material. Two more lengths of lath can be fixed in position as cart handles, and two discs of card, with rims and spokes painted in, can represent wheels. Fruit and vegetables can now be arranged, with price tags and a set of scales.

Use long lengths of handle cane, with supporting laths, to produce the framework of a large cornucopia. Card can now be fixed in position, with ties of string, to follow the whorls of the horn of plenty. Large sheets of newspaper liberally spread with paste are now laid over the card, and when dry paint is applied. Fruit and vegetables can now be positioned inside and cascading from the shell.

In a punnet or decorated cardboard box, arrange a selection of fruit and vegetables for display.
Gather together sprays of autumn leaves and fruit and nuts from the hedgerow and wood to make up a display.
Use nuts, fruit, leaves, etc., to make a collage picture of the autumn hedgerow.

Where a supply of straw is available, either from harvest festival sheaves or from an obliging farmer, use this material in a variety of ways.
(a) Flatten and split lengths of straw and with a strong adhesive, fix to black card to produce patterns or pictures.

(b) Flatten lengths of straw and fix pieces together in the form of stars. It is better, to begin with, to join lengths together as crosses with natural coloured cotton, and then superimpose one upon another. Lengths of straw can be varied, and the ends cut into points or V-shapes with knife or sharp scissors. Several stars can be used in a mobile. (see *Straw Stars* – Leisure Craft series.)

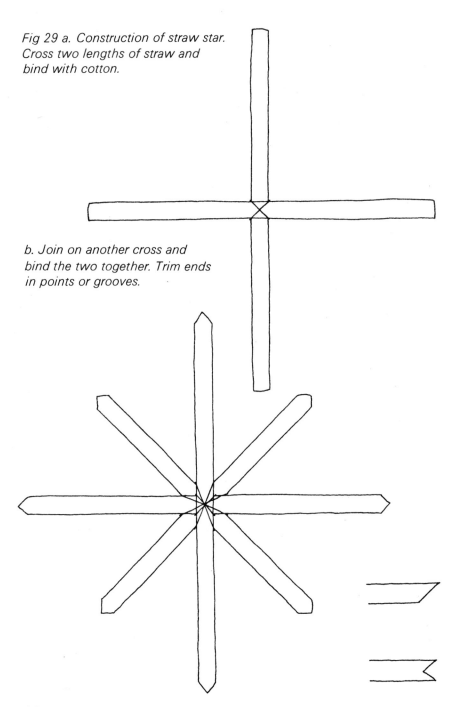

Fig 29 a. Construction of straw star. Cross two lengths of straw and bind with cotton.

b. Join on another cross and bind the two together. Trim ends in points or grooves.

(c) Make a corn dolly. Gatherers of the harvest from earliest times believed in the divine power of the corn. In Ancient Egypt, harvesting seemed like killing the gods, and so a ceremony was held in which the forgiveness of the Spirit of the Harvest was requested. The Passion of the Corn is described with amazing clarity and coherence in the John Barleycorn song, already mentioned. The making of the corn dolly is a fascinating exercise, and the various shapes and patterns appropriate to various counties of the British Isles, and countries in other parts of the world.

The following publications will be found of great interest. *A Golden Dolly, The Art, History and Mystery of Corn Dollies* by M. Lambeth (John Baker); *Decorative Straw Work* by Lettice Sandford and Philla Davis (Batsford); *Corn Dollies and How To Make Them* by Lettice Sandford and Philla Davis (Herefordshire Federation of Women's Institues, 43 Broad Street, Hereford). A simple form can be made by placing together a dozen straws which are about twenty-four inches long. If they are dry they can be made pliant by wrapping in a damp cloth overnight. The bundle should be doubled over, and at the bend, raffia should be used to tie a 'neck'. Another bundle of a dozen straws, about twelve inches long, should be pushed between the first bundle of straws just underneath the raffia tie. These are the arms, and another piece of raffia should be tied around the dolly, to hold these in place. Ties at the wrists will also keep the figure a neat one. More straw can be added as wings. Trimming with scissors will 'persuade' the dolly to stand. Straw plaiting can be done and lengths of this used for embellishments to the dolly or to make button-hole favours, with heads of wheat as centre pieces.

Make a model of a coal mine, diamond mine, oil well, and water well to illustrate the other treasures of the earth.

Search the vegetable box for unusual shaped vegetables and with simple embellishments — matchsticks, drawing pins, etc. — emphasise their likeness to animal and other forms.

Use fruit and vegetable forms to place together to represent human forms; birds and other animals. Suggest themes for development, e.g. The Race; The Boxing Match; The Wedding; Prehistoric Monsters.

Make a loaf of bread. Here is a recipe for Wholewheat Bread.
You will need:

1 oz (25g) Dried yeast
2 level tablespoons of brown sugar
1½ tablespoons of salt
3 lbs (1·5 kg) of plain wholemeal flour
1 oz (25 g) of lard
1½ pints (1 litre) of water

1 Whisk ½ pint (¼ litre) of water (at blood heat) with dried yeast and one teaspoonful of sugar. Leave for 15 minutes.
2 Rub lard into flour on pastry board or table. Make into a ring and press onto the board.
3 The rest of the water (also warmed), with salt and rest of sugar added, is poured into the ring, followed by the yeast mixture.
4 Gradually flick the flour from the outside of the ring into the centre, and mix it with the liquid. Make sure the ring does not break.
5 When sticky, knead in the rest of the flour. A smooth even texture should be obtained after 5 minutes.
6 Place the dough in a basin and cover with a damp tea towel. The basin should now be put in a warm place so that the dough can rise. After an hour, knead lightly on a floured board.
7 Now grease a baking tin and place in it about a quarter of the dough and leave in a warm place for another twenty minutes.
8 Now bake the bread for twenty minutes in a hot oven, 425°F (220°C) and then reduce heat to 400°F (205°C) for thirty minutes.
9 Tap base of bread, after removal from oven to see if bread is ready — a hollow sound indicates that it is.

Collect traditional and regional recipes for bread. Make these and arrange in a display with samples of the various grains.
Make a harvest loaf in the form of a wheatsheaf.

Collect and bottle fruit and vegetables.
Collect fruit, clean it, and make jam or jelly.

At St. Cuthbert's Church in Ackworth, a sheaf of corn is put outside the church to feed the birds. Build a bird table or post from which to provide food for birds near the school.

Links with other festivals
Autumn, Spring and Sowing; Good Neighbours; Harvest of the Sea;
Feast of Ceres – Goddess of Earth and Produce; Our Daily Bread;
Water.

CELEBRATING CHRISTMAS

The television comedian trying desperately to make us laugh on Boxing Day, might well end with the rejoinder that ' There are only 364 Shopping Days left till Christmas '. Such a remark may well begin to have a degree of truth to it, when one notices the early efforts of certain shops to decorate their windows for this great spending spree.

One might say that this section is in some way superfluous, because of all the possible occasions when schools could celebrate this is the one which they really do take to their hearts. In many cases the festival lasts for several days — often as long as three weeks. The only regret one might register, is where the preparation for it has gone on too long. Mid-November is quite early enough to start getting ready for Christmas (although planning details and choice of themes for carol programmes and plays will have been decided, and arrangements made to hire halls, equipment and even prepare costumes because of the almost universal desire to celebrate at this time of year — a feeling which goes back much farther in time than the birth of Jesus).

While one would want to preserve certain features of the traditional Christmas Celebration, it is important to try to inject some new life into the old formula. Not every child would write as one Boxgrove boy did last year, 'I never go to church at Christmas, because you know what is coming — the Christmas Story.' Nevertheless some long and serious thought should be given to the way Christmas will be celebrated at your school next year — rather than getting out the rather tattered nativity script and remarking 'I expect Mr. Jones will do the lights as usual.'

I think that a notebook is a useful thing for teachers to find in their Christmas stocking, and in it they might like to record those special features they notice during one Christmas for use on another. Shop windows, street arrangements, new carols, old neglected ones, the nativity play at another school, the folk carol service at the local church, the unusual Christmas card or wrapping paper they received, etc. The programme they saw on television, or heard on radio; the news item in the press, a newly-released record, etc. The ideas on these pages need not be slavishly followed, but adopted and adapted to suit the needs and conditions of the local situation.

Above all Christmas needs to be a joyful time. As one of my children wrote 'I like Christmas because it gives me such a happy filling'. Another child from a home with few advantages wrote, or rather said,

Plate 7 The Nativity Play.
(*Pace Ltd*)

for the teacher to write down:
  'I like Christmas Day because it is different. I'm happy, everybody
  is happy. I don't get into trouble. I come downstairs and I say
  'Wotcha Dad' and 'Wotcha Mum' and it stays like that all day.'

We all need Christmas.

INFORMATION AND INSPIRATION
Books
Matthew 1.18 – 2.23
Luke 1.5 – 2.38
John 1.1 – 1.15
Baker, Margaret: *Christmas Customs and Folklore.*

Bellson, H. and Morton, Phylis Digby: *The Christmas Book* (Sampson Low).

Braybrooke, Neville; *A Partridge in a pear tree* (Darton, Longman & Todd).

Buday, George: *The History of the Christmas Card* (Spring Books).

Collins, Philip: *English Christmas* (Gordon Frazer).

Goddard, H. S. W: *The Gardener's Christmas Book* (Collier Macmillan).

Grigson, O: *The Three Kings* (Gordon Frazer).

Hadfield, Miles and John: *The Twelve Days of Christmas* (Cassell).

Harrison, Michael: *The Story of Christmas* (Cassell).

Hole, C: *Christmas and Its Customs*.

Jones, M. A: *Tell Me About Christmas* (Collins).

Nettel, Reginald: *Santa Claus* (Gordon Frazer).

Posselt, E: *The World's Greatest Christmas Stories* (Worlds Work).

Reeves, J: *The Christmas Book* (Heinemann).

Sanson, W: *Christmas* (Weidenfeld and Nicolson).

Seymour, W. K: and Smith, John: *Happy Christmas* (Burke).

Walker, V. E: *Christmastide Stories* (NSSU).

Wyon, O: *The World's Christmas* (SCM).

Poetry

Belloc, Hilaire: *Noel*

Betjeman, J: *Christmas*

Chapman, Alexander J: *Christus Natus Est*

Causley, Charles: *Innocent's Song*

Chesterton, Frances: *The Children's Song of the Nativity*

Clare, John: *Christmas in a Village* and *December* (from 'Shepherd's Calendar')

de la Mare, W: *Mistletoe* and *A Ballad of Christmas*

Eliot, T. S: *The Journey of the Magi* and *A Song of Simeon*

Hardy, T: *The Oxen*

Hartnell, Phylis: *Bethlehem*

Kirkup, James: *Eve of Christmas*

Lee, Laurie: *Christmas Landscape*

Longfellow, H. W: *Three Kings Came Riding*

Milton, J: *Hymn on the Morning of Christ's Nativity*

Pasternak, Boris: *Star of the Nativity*

Press, John: *African Christmas*

Rodgers, W. R: *Carol*

Rossetti, C: *Christmas Daybreak*

Sansom, Clive: *Mary of Nazareth*

Shakespeare, W: *When Icicles Hang By The Wall*
Blow, Blow, Thou Winter Wind
Smith, J: *Somewhere Around Christmas*
Southwell, R: *Bethlehem*
Stevenson, R. L: *Christmas at Sea*
Young, A: *Christmas Day*

Music
(For listening)
Bach, J: *Christmas Oratorio*
Berlioz, Louis H: *L'Enfant du Christ*
Correlli: *Christmas Concerto*
Handel, G: *The Messiah*
The Faithful Shepherd
Honneger, Arthur: *Christmas Cantata*
Ireland, J: *Holy Boy*
Scarlatti, D: *A Christmas Cantata*
Schutz, H: *Christmas Oratorio*
Williams, Vaughan: *Fantasia on Christmas Carols*

There are many books of carols from which a selection can be made
to encourage one to look at Christmas from a particular direction
adopting such themes as 'The Seekers', 'Rejoice Again', 'King of Kings',
'Lord of the Universe', 'Lord of Man', 'Lord of Love', 'Lord of the Rich',
'Lord of the Poor', 'Lord of Life', 'Folk Nativity', 'Christ Born for The
World'. Once a title has been decided upon, then the carols are
chosen to illustrate it, and other activities — music, drama, movement,
art and craft can be integrated.

Oxford Book of Carols (O.U.P.).
The Penguin Book of Carols (Penguin).
Faith, Folk and Nativity (Galliard).
The Queensway Book of Carols (Evans).
The Kingsway Book of Carols (Evans).

Look in the catalogues of the various music publishers (see
bibliography) for well tried and tested, new and experimental work
for Christmas e.g. *A Festival of Folk Carols* by Anne Mendoza and
Joan Rimmer (Novello).

There are many good recordings of carols, arranged in a special way and/or sung by particular choirs. The purchase of one or more of these is a nice way of letting the school give itself a present.

This is a selection of suitable recordings:
Christmas Carols from Guildford Cathedral (E.M.I. MFP 1339),
Christmas Music from Westminster Abbey (E.M.I. CLP 3638).
Christmas Carols from St. Paul's (E.M.I. MFP 1264).
In Dulci Jubilo — Carols from Cambridge (S.S.D. 3634).
A Ceremony of Carols (Benjamin Britten) (Saga STX ID 5274).
Now Make We Merthe (Mediaeval carols) (Argo).

and a few E.P's:
Carols from Guildford (Abbey E 7628).
Carols from St. Albans (Abbey E 7625).
Carols from York Minster (Abbey E 7626).
Carols from New College (Abbey E 7627).

One of the Christmas activities might well be the recording of a programme of carols by the choir or the whole school. Such a prospect does wonders to raise the quality of the singing. It is possible to have such a tape of music dubbed onto a record. One such firm which will perform this service is Deroy Sound Services, High Bank, Hawk Street, Carnforth, Lancs.

In certain areas, records of such a concert will be made by a local firm provided a certain number of sales can be guaranteed. Usually there are sufficient parents willing to buy this unique kind of school souvenir.

Other kinds of music abound at Christmas too. Some interesting material will be found on Topic Record, *Songs of Christmas* and Topic Record 12T316, *Frost and Fire*. Such material also takes us back to the times before Christ when there were feasts of light, fire festivals, Saturnalia and other sun worshipping pagan activities linked to the winter solstice.

Every year the pop world throws up some song which gets a 12-day airing and is usually lost without trace. Certain themes survive — *White Christmas, Rudolph the Red-Nosed Reindeer, Jingle Bells,* and the Christmas party is the place for these if everyone is not

suffering from a surfeit of jelly.
Record: *The Witnesses,* Clive Sanson (Argo DA 87 – Also relevant to Easter).

Films
The Prince of Peace (Rank Films).
A Charles Dickens Christmas (Rank Films).
Early One Morning (Christmas Day in Sweden) (Rank Films).

Excursions and other activities
To a local church or cathedral to take part in a Christmas Service.
To make up a party to attend a church service at midnight on Christmas Eve (with parents' permission and with the parents too).
To prepare a carol programme and tour the local streets, collecting for some agreed good cause. Hospitals, old people's homes, etc.
Another school may well welcome such a visit especially where there is an opportunity to participate.
A visit to places in the town or city where the local authority or organisations have arranged to make a special display.
Visit to a large shopping area to see the Christmas display and any joint enterprise they have engaged in.
Visit a local Post Office sorting office to see the volume of extra work and how this is coped with.
Organise a visit to a traditional pantomime. Those schools in or near London often have a good choice with perennial favourites like *Wind in the Willows.*
Visit The Planetarium, London to see the programme 'Star of Bethlehem'.

CREATIVE ACTIVITIES
Writing
In services of readings and carols at Christmas time, various texts forecast and record the events which are being celebrated at this time. A selection can be made from these.
Genesis 3 vv 8-13, 15-18, 22-24 – The original sin of Adam and Eve.
Genesis 17 vv 1-8 – God's promise to Abraham.
Genesis 22 vv 15-18 – Abraham does not withold his only son.
Isaiah 7 v 14 – The virgin birth is foretold.

154

Isaiah 9 v 2, 6 & 7 – Jesus's birth is foretold.
Isaiah 11 v 1-3, 4, 6-9 – Telling of what kind of person Jesus will be.
Isaiah 40 vv 1-5, 9-11 – Prepare the way.
Isaiah 52 vv 7-10 – The Promise of things to come.
Micah 5 vv 2-4 – Informing the people of the coming of Christ.
St. Luke I vv 26-35, 38 – The Angel appears to Mary.
St. Luke 2 vv 1, 3-7 – The Roman decree. Mary and Joseph go to
    Bethlehem.
St. Luke 2 vv 8-16 – The Shepherds are summoned.
St. Matthew 2 vv I-II – The Wise Men arrive.
St. John 1 vv 1-14 The Word Was Made Flesh.

Produce a newsheet of the events leading up to and following the
birth of Jesus. Illustrate this with drawings.

Take the readings of the story and re-compose them so that a
seven-year-old child could understand. The following reading
(John 1: 1-14) was prepared by members of a fourth year Junior
class and it has become part of the Boxgrove Readings.
   When the world was made, God was the builder. God was there
   already, and His Spirit, and His son Jesus, who lived with Him in
   Heaven not on earth.

   Jesus lived with God, and was part of Him until he was needed upon
   earth. He always was part of God until his life on earth was ended
   and afterwards he went back to heaven again to live with God.
   Jesus was always here and is still here today and will always be
   here and in heaven as well.

   There was a man called John who was the cousin of Jesus, born a
   little while before Him. God sent him to tell everyone of the coming
   of Jesus who was to be king for ever. He was a messenger to tell
   everyone to be ready for Jesus who would follow him and help
   people and cure people and give them new faith and new life.
   Jesus came and people thought he was an ordinary man. He came
   to earth and the people on earth would not believe he was the son
   of God; but the people who did believe he was telling them the
   truth and who followed him, he promised would go to heaven to be
   near God and himself for ever.

   So God became a human being and came to live on earth amongst
   men.

You are a young attendant at the court of King Herod. Tell the story of the arrival of the Wise Men and what happened when the King realised that they would not return.

Compose a lullaby for Mary to sing to her babe.

Write a poem about the Shepherds and their fear, and wonder at the events of that night.

Compose a short refrain which could be used during a carol service.

Compose a short refrain and set it to music composed on tuned instruments. Use this after readings at a carol service. Here is an example, taken from a service for which the theme was 'King of Kings'. (See page 175 for the music)

> Baby Born in Bethlehem's Manger
> Born A King, Born A King
> Praise and Glory Let Us Bring.

Coloured transparencies of paintings can be purchased from various Art Galleries. The National Art Gallery, Trafalgar Square, London, W.C.1 has a very large catalogue of pictures including many nativity scenes. These can be bought or hired very cheaply. Write a linking commentary for a set of 40 slides telling the story of the Nativity.

Alternatively prepare a programme of carols which tell the story of the birth of Jesus. Look carefully at the content of each hymn or song and decide upon a simple illustration with a group of children who are then commissioned to paint the pictures. These are then photographed to produce coloured transparencies. Once again a commentary is required and two rehearsals with pictures back projected (so that the choir can get used to them and get on with the singing!) Here is the schedule produced by a dozen children working on this assignment. As well as these new 'masters', transparencies from the previous year's Infant Nativity play were projected to act in certain cases as the introductory pictures.

Scenario for a Folk Nativity

Carol, Hymn or song	Supporting pictures
1 Magnificat	Women, kneeling in prayer – hands upheld – a great light shining from above.
2 No Room At The Inn (5 verses)	(a) Mary and Joseph approaching Bethlehem (with donkey).

		(b) At the door of a great house.
		(c) Close up of hostess refusing Mary and Joseph lodging.
		(d) Hostess points way to stable.
		(e) Inside stable. Confusion — beggars, animals. Central figure, Mary — calm and serene.
3	Mary's view	Picture of Mary with her baby. Large portrait from lap upwards.
4	Sing and Rejoice	Sea of faces with large open mouths. Different ages and nationalities.
5	Rise Up Shepherd	One shepherd with large flock. Distant view of village.
6	Go Tell it On The Mountain	Shepherds around the crib.
7	The Virgin Mary Had a Baby Boy	A Baby in swaddling clothes.
8	To Jesus	Three very wise old men.
9	Every Star Shall Sing A Carol	A Picture of the universe with stars and planets.
10	Children Go Where I send You	Composite picture with line drawings of each of the people mentioned, e.g. Four at the door, Five Who Came Back Alive. (During the refrain, which is an accumulator, each of the items is picked out with a torchlight.)

The last carol was used to evacuate the church at the end of the church, as class after class left, singing their way into the street.

Drama and movement

Perform the story of the nativity using the New Testament to provide the words and action.

Perform the story of the nativity as though it were happening today, in your own locality.

Holly From The Bongs by Alan Garner and Roger Hill (Collins) provides an interesting full treatment of the making of a Nativity Play.

Refer to *Seven Miracle Plays* by Alex Franklin (Oxford U. Press) or other sources and perform one of these plays.

Act the story of Amahl and the Night Visitors (with or without the music by Gian-Carlo Menotti).
Perform the operetta *Herod Do Your Worst* by Bryan and Kelly. (Listen also to the *Play of Herod,* 12th century drama on Nonesuch H.7 1181.)
Perform traditional Mummers Play of St. George and the Dragon.
From *Christmas Stories Around The World* by Lois Johnson (Warne) and *The Long Christmas* by Ruth Sawyer (Bodley Head) select items for performance.

Choose a traditional pantomime to cast and act.

Look for interesting Christmas stories in well known tales to provide material for a playlet, puppet play, shadow play or mime e.g. from Charles Dickens — Bob Cratchet's Christmas from *The Christmas Carol;* Paddington Bear's Christmas from Michael Bond's *More About Paddington* (Collins), Christmas Underground from Kenneth Grahame's *Wind in the Willows; The Thieves Who Couldn't Help Sneezing* by Thomas Hardy.
Consult *The Christmas Drama Book* edited by Irene Gass (Harrap) and select suitable plays to perform or adapt.
Read *Christmas in the Market Place* translated by E. Crosier (Muller) and perform the play.
Using Tchaikovsky's music, tell the story of The Nutcracker in drama and movement.

Refer to various sources of information available and discuss the facts and fantasies of the story of St. Nicholas, and improvise a play.
Read *The Flowering Hawthorn* by Hugh Ross Williamson (Peter Davies) which tells the legend and history connected with the famous thorn of Glastonbury. Create a play from this story about Joseph of Arimathea.

Learn The Cherry Tree Carol and mime the story to the singing of it.

Read the story of Simeon (St. Luke vv 26-38) and act the events described.

Tell the story of the custom of wassailing. Prepare a bowl of 'lambswool' — put whipped cream, sugar and spices in boiling ale (for this substitute a mineral water) and then add roasted apples

('When roasted crabs hiss in the bowl'). Decorate the bowl with ribbons and garlands, and carry around from farm to farm until everyone has toasted the season. On the eve of Epiphany the trees are wassailed by sprinkling them from the bowl. Branches are pulled down to suggest they are laden with fruit and sacks are 'filled' with the harvest they hope will come.

Create a Christmas scene from the Middle Ages when the Abbot of Unreason or the Lord of Misrule took over for twelve anarchic days and the roles of authority were reversed.

Discover all you can of the Russian legend of Baboushka who was invited to make the journey to Bethlehem, but who said she had work to do and so was too late. Prepare this story as a shadow play, with spoken dialogue.

Art
Produce a number of pictures, e.g. Bethlehem, the Hills, a Seaport and arrange these in a central place in the school — hall or corridor — and ask everyone to contribute figures and buildings until the nativity story is complete.

Design a programme for a Christmas Concert, illustrating its contents.

Make a large advent calendar, with sections to open each day to reveal symbols of Christmas and Winter. Classes in turn can be responsible for opening the dated doors.

Provide a variety of materials and ask for cards, calendars, gift tags to be designed.

Using materials, crêpe paper, etc., make a collage picture of Father Christmas and his reindeer. Additional packages in two and three dimensions can be added.

Collect Christmas cards which are illustrated by religious imagery. An appeal to *The Sunday Times* or *The Observer* for such cards to be sent to a school after Christmas brings a good response. One does not need to profess a strong religious belief, and yet is likely to be profoundly moved by the pictures of the Madonna and Child. Most of the great artists of the world (and many musicians and writers too) have found this theme an immensely challenging one. Let the children study these pictures and after an interval of time, ask them to draw and colour what they feel about this stable scene.

Use crayon or paint to make a picture of the Three Wise Men being given an audience by King Herod.

Draw and colour a picture of the inside or outside of a busy shop at Christmas time.

Craft
Make a crib scene, with figures constructed of pipe cleaners, and dressed in scrap fabrics. (See *Let's Make a Christmas Crib,* Mills and Boon, and *Christmas Crib* – Leisure Crafts.)

Research into menus for great Christmas feasts of the past and model these in papier mâché and arrange on a table with linen, appropriate crockery and cutlery of the period (modelled if necessary).

For the Christmas feast, make up table decorations to fit in with a particular theme, e.g. A Scottish Christmas; Frost and Fire. Plaster of Paris is useful to pour into metal lid moulds, so that candles, holly leaves, Christmas baubles, etc. can be held in place. Plaster of Paris can also be poured over sections of log, and just before the material sets, candles holly twigs with leaves and berries can be positioned. (Several layers of newspaper are needed on tables and the floor when plaster is being used and on no account should the waste material be put down the sink.)

Using cones of paper, make up the main shapes of angels – add arms and wings. Suspend these in a place appropriate to their size.

On a ring, made up of several layers of pliable wire (S.W.G. 18) make up an Advent wreath of ivy, holly and moss. Open out wire loops in the wreath to take four large candles. Light these on the four weeks before Christmas.
Take a set of candles, and with handicraft knives carve a set of heads of figures in the nativity scene.

160

Fig 30 Conical forms used for making paper angels.

Decorate a tree inside, and a tree outside the building. Consider what materials to use to withstand the wintry weather. (Consult an electrician before running a cable outside to power lights.)

Decorate a number of hoops joined together and add other ornaments to suspend from the ceiling. (See *Christmas Decorations* by Alison Liley (Mills and Boon) .)

Collect sprays of box, holly, mistletoe, fir and laurel and make up a Christmas arrangement.

Collect the ingredients for a Christmas Cake, Christmas pudding —
or (more modestly) mince pies. Prepare these to a traditional recipe,
cook — and enjoy them.

Make up separate appliqué panels for each of the Three Wise Men.

If a long display panel is available, design a low relief picture of the
arrival of the Magi in Bethlehem. Use paper sculpture techniques with
pieces of card, fixing these in place with a staple.

With Polystyrene tiles bought from a do-it-yourself shop or pieces of
this material begged from radio and television shops, make up
Christmas shapes — in the form of icicles and snow flakes. A sharp
knife cuts this material and so does a piece of metal, e.g. and old
knife, warmed in a flame. A special tool costing approximately 50 pence
can be bought from handicraft shops. This is battery operated and a
heated wire cuts easily through the Polystyrene. The same kind of
shop will sell you a Polystyrene adhesive. The ink from felt pens has a
chemical action on Polystyrene and some low relief sculpting can
be attempted with them.

Where supervision is available throughout the operation, decorative
candle making can be introduced. Paraffin wax can be bought from
very large chemists (e.g. Boots). White candles can be bought from
a grocer and melted down to extract the wick. Cotton yarn can be used
for the wick, which is the material used to make pyjama cords.

The wax is melted over a low heat in an old saucepan, and at this point
colouring can be added. For this, wax crayons or coloured birthday
candles are suitable. Tins, plastic containers which are cylindrical in
shape, and small dishes make suitable moulds. Grease the mould with
cooking oil and place it ready on a table well covered with paper.
Tie a small weight e.g. a nut or a button, to the wick and position
this in the centre of the mould. Pour in the wax holding the end of
wick in a central position. As the candle wax sets, a well will appear
in the top around the wick. Top this up with more hot wax, and at
this point pass the top end of the wick through a carboard disc
already prepared, and leave the process of cooling to continue for as
much as twelve hours. Wax of different colours can be added to produce
rings providing that cooling is allowed to take place between each
pouring.

Gentle tapping should make it easy to remove the candle from its mould but where there is resistance, dip the container into hot water to melt the outer layers. In the case of tin cans, the bottom should be cut around and the candle pressed through.

Where spherical shapes are desired, identical shapes can be cast in semi-circular moulds and the flat faces should be warmed slightly and pressed together. There is lots of room for experiment in this craft and scope for displaying and using the candles in a variety of carefully selected dishes.

Candle-Makers Supplies, 4 Beaconsfield Terrace Road, off Blythe Road, London, W.14, supply all materials required for this craft – wax, dyes, mould, seal and perfumes.

Use straw (milk straws if no others have been held over from a Harvest Celebration) to make straw angels (see All Is Safely Gathered In section).

Links with other festivals
Epiphany; Candlemas; Easter; Winter; Saturnalia.

POSTSCRIPT

After a celebration, thanks to all concerned would seem to be in order. One is always hopeful that it will have been thought of as an exciting occasion: it will certainly have been a demanding one. The director may like to say his word of thanks – including a reminder of what has been celebrated – but he may wish to do this in the calmer atmosphere of the following day, and leave it to a guest to provide a few words of appreciation.

There will have been a hard working task force, responsible for setting out staging, chairs, scenery, etc; there is likely to be just as great a need for people to put the place in order again. Care will be needed to be taken of costumes, props, tapes, records, etc. and this responsibility should be delegated during the planning stage.

Cups of tea will be appreciated and if some small extra can be included, with some direct link with the theme, then so much the better. A Christmas cake bedecked in the school colours would go down well after the Celebration of Carols; some Tea Time Assorted biscuits and a box of After-Eight Chocolates would resuscitate those exhausted after their efforts in the Time Festival; iced, heart-shaped biscuits, decorated with the sweets from the confectioner, called Love Hearts, will probably raise something of a smile.

Some effort should be made to make a record of the activities of the Celebration. Some of the dramatic items might be filmed on 8mm stock; songs and choral speech can be taped; pictures and models can be photographed on 35mm colour transparencies. Of course it may not be appropriate to carry out any of these activities during the Celebration, because of lighting and acoustical problems, and in any case the adjustment of lights or microphone positions would be a distraction and an annoyance not only to the participants but also the children who are forming the audience for that section of the proceedings. Far better to arrange for the particular items to be presented with filming, or tape recording in mind. Where the press have been invited, a cutting from the local newspaper – plus a photograph, and a copy of the programme, can be fixed into the school album. Indulgent parents may also take photographs in black and white or colour, and a print from their negatives is useful for the school archives.

It is useful to prepare a book or a file on each festival, with copies of the songs, poems, sources of stories, etc. and make space and time to add ideas subsequently discovered or thought up, because within each celebration there are the ingredients or starting points for others. In the case of my *Book of Festivals*, I have found staff referring to it for material for use in class projects, and for this reason too it is important to continue to explore and expand the chosen theme.

While it is important that every child and every class makes a contribution to a celebration, it would be equally splendid if each took something from the situation. One class might like to record their impressions in words and pictures and call it 'Our Book of the King of Tonga's Visit' while another might prepare a frieze illustrating their work on 'Good Neighbours', including in it receipts, and letters received in response to their practical aid, etc. One class might take the May Festival as an initial experience for a project on Fairs and Markets.

From a festival may spring the suggestion that something permanent might be obtained. Our May Fair raised money for the purchase of a carpet for the library – in fact in many children's minds, this celebration was known as the Carpet Fair. We had a visit from the Education Sub-Committee prior to this celebration and one person with a particular interest in this type of activity was very curious about this Carpet Fair, imagining that we had resurrected some ancient Trade Fair. We bought a replica of an old English broadsword in Battle, Sussex, during the 1066 Celebration, and many times since the anniversary year, this has been 'used' in the school. Following the Flower Festival we have placed a regular weekly order with the florist to supplement those blooms brought in by the children.

At the end of each year, the leavers like to include a reprise on certain selected items from those celebrations in which they have taken part in a kind of Festival of Festivals. Since some of the memorable features of events are from occasions as much as five or six years previously, yet another interesting reminder is provided, and continuity of celebrations and festivals assured.

We feel festivals are an important part of our way of life — a necessary part of the year looked on in the same light as our hardworking forebears of earlier times saw their 'holidays'. One of our young first year girls sums this up adequately even if a trifle lacking in the niceties of English grammar,

'I like festivals Because of the Joy people get out of it. Some people think a Festival is very mad. But I and a Lot of People think it is a very good Idea.'

There is a need for magic and invention, and things much larger than life, to be included in school life to help each child understand his surroundings. There is a need too, for a little madness to keep us sane for as Prospero observes in *The Tempest:*

Be cheerful sir:
Our revels now are ended; these our actors
As I foretold you, were all spirits and
Are melted into air, into thin air:
And, like the baseless fabric of this vision
The cloud capp'd towers, the gorgeous palaces,
The solemn temples, the great globe itself,
Yea, all which it inherit, shall dissolve,
And like this insubstantial pageant faded,
Leave not a rack behind: We are such stuff
As dreams are made on, and our little life
Is rounded with a sleep.

And soon we are back again in the workaday world, but perhaps in a short while, thoughts can again turn to Festivals and Celebrations and invitations can be sent to colleagues just as once again Prospero observes almost immediately after the speech above.

'Come, with a thought: I thank you.'

APPENDIX 1 SOUNDS FOR CELEBRATIONS

Festivals and celebrations will usually include music in a variety of forms, and this should be chosen and created both with the theme in mind and the relative ease with which it can be played and enjoyed both by the participants and the audience.

In the case of songs, the piano is not the only instrument which can be used for accompaniment. The guitar is being increasingly used, but even this should not be over exposed. Unaccompanied singing makes a refreshing change too. If the children in a school have had a good diet of song, then they should be ready by the upper junior age to increase their range, and be introduced to two-part work and other work with more complicated structures. Where opportunities can be found in the primary school, instrumental skills, e.g. on string instruments, can be introduced without removing the activity or the compositions outside the classroom. The recorder is a simple instrument to introduce into the primary field and by the end of this phase of education, the treble and tenor versions of the instrument should be put in the hands of the most promising pupils, so that there is variety in the 'orchestra'.

The human voice can be used in yet another way, by the development of the saying of word rhythms, and by combining this with other sounds such as claps, thigh slaps, clicks, and foot stamps. Gradually untuned and tuned percussion instruments can be introduced, so that creative music can be developed to support drama, or movement work or stand in its own right.

In-service courses are invaluable in introducing non-specialists to this type of creative activity. Further help is available from two records – *Music For Children,* Columbia CX 1549/1550 featuring the work of Carl Orff, Gunild Keetman and Walter Jellinek, and books, *Music for Children 1-4* by Carl Orff translated by Margaret Murray

(Schotts), Orff Schulwerk – *Teacher Manual* (Schott) and *Choral Method* by Zoltan Kodaly 18 titles (Boosey and Hawkes).

Where funds are available for buying instruments, quality should be the main criteria and Studio 49 equipment should satisfy everyone. Order of purchasing might be as follows:
Glockenspiel (Soprano)
Xylophone (Alto)
Xylophone (Soprano)
Metallophone (Alto)
Glockenspiel (Alto)

Base metallophones and xylophones are expensive, but if one received a windfall from somewhere – it couldn't be better spent than on one of those. By choosing diatonic instruments (with notes limited to the the scale prevailing at the moment) rather than chromatic – money is saved. Once again Studio 49 produce the best non-pitched percussion instruments and tambours, tambourines, bells, castanets, claves, cymbals, maraccas and triangles should be purchased in as great a quantity as one can afford.

In addition, and not merely out of expediency, musical instruments can be manufactured in the classroom, decorated and used.

Many of these are made from scrap or cheap material and once an introduction is made, the children should be encouraged to develop their own particular type of rhythm instrument.

SHAKERS

Take a small tin with a fitted lid. Pierce a hole in the lid, just big enough for a small length of dowel rod to pass through. Fix a nail through the tin into the rod to secure it. Quarter fill the tin with dried peas, small gravel, etc., refix the lid and seal with Sellotape. A larger shaker can be made by inflating a balloon and covering it with about half a dozen layers of papier mâché. When dry puncture the balloon, and with a funnel pour in a small quantity of rice grains and fit a dowel rod into the hole. Fix a small piece of Plasticine over the dowel rod where it enters the balloon and cover this with several layers of papier mâché to seal. An old electric light bulb can be covered completely with papier mâché in the same way, and when dry given a sharp tap to break the glass inside, which will create sound when the instrument is shaken.

A collection of crown corks can be made, and each punctured in the centre with a large nail. These can be attached to a short stick for shaking or to a long one, which can be banged on the floor. Smaller nails should be used when constructing this lagerphone. Yet another way to use these crown corks is to suspend them across a V-shaped piece of branchwood. Most boys can identify a catapult shape when required.

If the local toyshop can supply small jingle bells, a number of these can be sewn onto a piece of carpet or other stout material and this fixed to each end of a 5-inch (13-cm) piece of dowel rod.

SCRAPERS
Pieces of wood, 4" x 2" x 1" (102 x 51 x 25mm) can be covered with coarse glass-paper, using drawing pins to secure. Pairs of these rubbed together make a very pleasing sound.

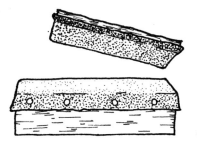

Fig 31 Glasspaper music blocks.

A guiro is made by taking a section of bamboo and carefully filing a series of grooves in it. A small smooth stick can then be trailed up and down to produce a rhythmic clicking sound.

Fig 32 A guiro made from a section of bamboo with a series of grooves filed along one side. A smooth stick trailed along these grooves will produce a graduated noise.

BEATERS AND BANGERS

Since all sounds have a potential musical quality about them, we must experiment and suggest ways in which they can be organised to create musical structures. A variety of materials, should be tried, e.g. glass, wood, metal, etc. A sound box can be made simply by nailing together four pieces of wood in a rectangular form. Two strips of foam rubber should be glued along the two long edges, and on these the various materials should be tried. Children will soon come to various conclusions about the quality of the sound produced, but also the relation between the size of it and the note produced. This is not such a far step to creating an effective xylophone, with metal or wooden pieces cut to lengths which will produce a scale.

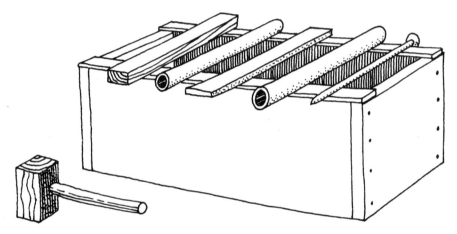

Fig 33 A sound box to establish sound produced from various materials.

Similarly a set of chimes can be manufactured by suspending cut lengths of pipe under a low shelf. Some care needs to be taken with the cutting of the pipes. Providing the material is standard throughout, then the pipes can be measured to length, e.g. a scale of eight notes (in D major) can be produced with pipes (or wooden blocks which measure 8″, $8\frac{3}{8}$″, $9\frac{1}{4}$″, $9\frac{5}{8}$″, $10\frac{1}{4}$″, $10\frac{3}{4}$″, $11\frac{1}{2}$″ and $12\frac{1}{2}$″. Incidentally, strikers can be quite simply made by sticking a short length of cane into a wooden ball, which has had a small hole bored into it.

Another form of tuned percussion can be created by assembling a series of identical bottles and filling them partly with water so that they will produce a scale when struck in turn. If they are to be kept for any length of time, corking will be needed to prevent evaporation.

Drums can also be manufactured and decorated most attractively to fit in with an African scene for example. A length of thin wood veneer should be bent into a cylinder and fixed into this position.

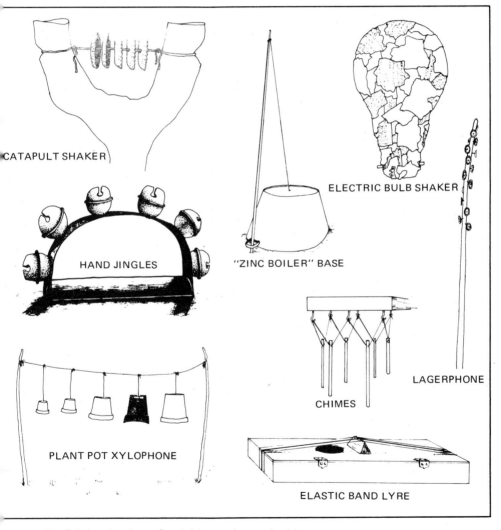

CATAPULT SHAKER

ELECTRIC BULB SHAKER

HAND JINGLES

"ZINC BOILER" BASE

LAGERPHONE

CHIMES

PLANT POT XYLOPHONE

ELASTIC BAND LYRE

Fig 34 A selection of quickly-made musical instruments.
By courtesy of Evans Brothers Limited.

A staple gun is useful for this, bending over the staples, after firing them through. A wide band of cellulose tape will reinforce the joint. Try two methods of making a skin. Select a large sheet of stout cartridge paper and immerse it in water for five minutes. Allow the excess water to drip off and then lay it on the open end of the drum. Cut with scissors from the outside edge towards the centre but stop short fractionally before the edge of the cylinder. Use thick polycell paste to stick these flaps down on the outside edge of the drum, moving from one side to the other of the instrument and pulling the paper as tightly as possible – without tearing of course. A band of cartridge paper can be stuck around the edge to make a neater finish and to help secure the 'skin'. Alternatively, tear the cartridge paper into strips about 2 inches wide (51mm) and lay these across the other end of the drum, sticking the end into place. All pieces will pass over the centre, and each is glued throughout its length. This end of the drum will have a reinforced head at the centre and will produce a different note from the other end. In drying, the skins will both become much tighter. The fingers or a felt-headed stick should be used to beat the rhythm.

PLUCKERS AND TWANGERS

In the immediate post-war years the skiffle groups showed their enterprise in raiding the kitchen and wash house for their raw materials. The zinc boiler base was a typical example of this type of instant instrument. A broomshank is wedged into the handle of an upturned zinc boiler. A string is attached by a stick through the bottom of the boiler at the lower end to the top of broomstick at the other. By bending the stick backwards and forwards a different note is produced.

A cigar box can be transformed into a simple stringed instrument. A hole should be cut in the lid to allow the sound to resonate. A small triangular section of wood should be glued to the lid parallel to the shorter sides. Elastic bands of varying thicknesses should now be placed around the length of the box and over the bridge. The fingers are used to pluck the bands.

A more sophisticated instrument which we might call a lyre can be developed from the cigar box idea. A trapezoid shape should be built up with short lengths of timber and a top and bottom cut from

3-ply wood pinned and glued into position. A sound hole or holes should be cut (with a fret saw) before fixing the top, of course. Nails should be fixed at intervals along the non-parallel sides and to these, lengths of guitar or violin strings should be tied as tightly as possible. A short length of wood, e.g. an old ruler, can now be inserted beneath all the strings, and rotated until it is in the upright position, so making the strings very taut. Fingers or a plectrum can be used to pluck the lyre strings.

BOOKS

There are a number of books and publications which are most useful for help in instrument manufacture and their playing.

Addison, Richard: *Begin Making Music* (Holmes McDougall).
           Make Music (Holmes McDougall).

Blocksidge, K. M: *Making Musical Apparatus and Instruments for use in Nursery and Infants Schools* (Nursery School Association pamphlet No. 71).

Bulman, William M: *Music in Action* (The Sound of the Sea, The Sound of the City, The Sound of the Country, Teacher's Book – Rupert Hart Davis).

Clemens, G: *Making Music* (Longmans).

Kettlekamp, Larry: *Drums, Rattles and Bells* (Wheaton).

Mandell, Muriel and Wood Robert E: *Make your Own Musical Instruments* (Sterling Publishing Co., New York).

Roberts, Ronald: *Make Your Own Musical Instruments* (Dryad Press).

Self, G: *New Sounds in Glass* (Universal Edition).

Williams, P. H. M: *Lively Craft Cards, Set 2* (illustrated instructions for making simple instruments – Mills and Boon).

MUSIC PUBLISHERS

Augener, 148 Charing Cross Road, London, W.C.2.
Boosey and Hawkes, 295 Regent Street, London, W.2.
Chappell, 50 New Bond Street, London, W.1.
Curwen, 29 Maiden Lane, London, W.C.2.
Galliard, 148 Charing Cross Road, London, W.C.2.
Novello & Co. Ltd., Borough Green, Sevenoaks, Kent.
Oxford University Press, 44 Conduit Street, London, W.1.
Paxton & Co., 36 Dean Street, London, W.1.
Schott, 48 Great Marlborough Street, London, W.1.

RECORD COMPANIES AND AGENTS

Below is information about record companies and agents who handle records which are likely to be of particular use to schools but which may not be available for inspection in record shops.

Abbey (poetry, songs, organ music, etc.).

Argo Record Company, 115 Fulham Road, London, S.W.3. (poetry, drama, prose).

Audio Impact, 11 St. George Street, Hanover Square, London, W.1. (Handles records from Abbey, Jupiter, Era, Saydisc).

BBC Radio Enterprises, Villiers House, Haven Green, London, W.5. (Issues records of rare, unusual and unexpected broadcasts.)

Caedmon, Stanhope House, Stanhope Place, London, E.W.2. (Plays, poems, prose, etc.)

Collet's, 70 New Oxford Street, London, W.1. (Records of folk songs, magazines, songbooks, etc.)

Delyse Envoy Records, ATV House, 17 Great Cumberland Place, London, W.1. (Songs, instrumental music, military bands, folk music, etc.)

Discourses Ltd., 10a High Street, Tunbridge Wells, Kent. (Handles BBC recordings, drama, natural history, poetry, prose, songs.)

English Folk Dance and Song Society, Cecil Sharp House, 2 Regent's Park Road, London, N.W.1. (Records, songs, information on customs, festivals, etc.).

Era Records (Plays, readings, etc.).

Jupiter Recordings, 140 Kensington Church Street, London, W.8 (Poetry recordings, prose, music and musical appreciations.)

Leader Sound Ltd., 5 North Villas, London, N.W.1. (Leader and Trailer records, songs.)

McGraw-Hill Spoken Arts, Maidenhead, Berkshire. (Drama, poems, prose, folk and other songs.)

Paxton & Co., Ltd., 36–38 Dean Street, London, W.1. (Records for play productions, singing games, dances, etc.)

Shell (from Discourses Ltd.). (Records of bird songs and other sounds of the countryside.)

Topic Records Ltd., 27 Nassington Road, London, N.W.3. (Folksongs, collections of music, regional, national and international. Free leaflets, *Topics in History, Topics for Juniors, Folk Songs in School, Folk Song and Ballad in the English lesson.* Folk music, religion and quarterly reports.)

Transatlantic and Xtra Records, 72 Heath Street, London, N.W.3.

Chris Welland Records Ltd., 6 Lewisham Way, London, S.E.14. (Handles records by the recording companies listed here.)

SOUND EFFECTS

In addition to making music, there are likely to be a number of occasions when sound effects are required during a festival to create a more realistic situation. Where possible it is better to tape-record such effects, and splice them together in correct order, separated by a piece of coloured leader tape, with a careful note taken of the counter number of the beginning and the end of the recording revolutions on the *tape recorder you are going to use at the performance.* Where the tape recorder has the appropriate cut-out device, a piece of magnetic foil tape can be inserted, so that the machine will stop itself at the end of the section. Where some continuous sound is required — storm effects, monk's plain song, bird song — a short length of tape can be made up and this cut and spliced into a loop. This can then be passed through the sound head and two empty spools as guides, and then around a cotton reel, spinning freely on a nail fixed in a block of wood. Alternatively, the tape can pass around a jar of sand or water, providing the tape can be kept taut enough to travel along in a horizontal path.

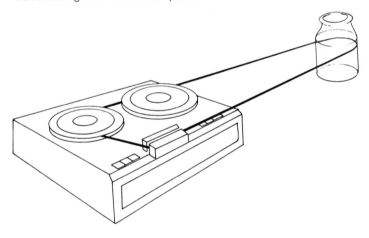

Fig 35 Running a tape loop on the tape recorder when one continuous sound is required.

The unexpected thing about many sound effects is that so many of them have to be simulated. It is not just the greater availability of coconut shells than horses, but the former rhythmically rattled on a table sound more like the canter and gallop of horses than the real thing recorded at the local stables.

Footsteps, for walking, marching and running, can be achieved by shaking a box half-filled with gravel or dried peas.

The same dried peas placed on top of a drum skin, and 'swished' backwards and forwards will take one to the seashore very quickly. If you get one of the children to drive a lot of nails into a box from the base and then tilt the box, with dried peas in it, the rain will begin to fall. A heavier shower will result when rice is dropped onto a drum.

If one requires wind effects, then the human voice can be tried – while for thunder a large sheet of cardboard, flexed backwards and forwards should suffice.

Paper crumbled in front of the microphone can suggest the sound of fire, but it is a good idea to try different grades of paper, and distances from the microphone. Sometimes the effect of playing back at half the speed, will produce a better sound.
A piece of cane thwacked onto a cushion, will give a good indication of rifle fire, and so on.

There are of course a number of records on the market which will provide almost any type of sound effect required. It is a good idea to tape-record even from these records, fading in and out after the correct amount of sound has been selected. Here is a list of some of the recordings available to date and as new material becomes available it is a good plan to make a note of it for future reference.

Bird songs
The Farm and Garden, HMV 7 EG 8923.
Heath, Common, Fields, and Hedgerow, HMV 7 EG 8926/8.
Woodland, Copse and Wet Habitats, HMV 7 EG 8929/31.
Songs of British Birds 1, HMV 7 EG 8315.
Songs of British Birds 2, HMV 7 EG 8316.
Wild Fowl Calling, HMV 7 EG 8964.
A Tapestry of British Bird Song, CLP 1723.
Sound of the Countryside, Abbey 39/9.

Shell nature records
(produced by Discourses Ltd.)
Sounds of the Countryside DCL 700.
Sea Birds   DCL 701.
Garden and Park Birds   DCL 702.
Woodland Birds   DCL 703.
Estuary Birds   DCL 704.
Field and Open Countryside Birds DCL 705.
Moor and Heath Birds   DCL 706.
Marsh and Riverside Birds DCL 707.
The Countryside Sings   DCL 751.

Dandy records
Real Train DB7
Real Farm Sounds DB100.
Real Bird Sounds DB101.
Real Bell Sounds DB103.

Sound effects from HMV
Space Ships & Ghosts 7FX15.
Aeroplanes   7FX13.
Air Raid   7FX 1.
Birds   7FX11 .
Car Effects   7FX 2.
Church Bells   7FX 3.
Demolition   7FX14.
Dogs   7FX 4.
Horses   7FX 5.
Ships and Rain   7FX 7.
Sea Effects   7FX 6
Street Noises   7FX12.
Thunderstorms   7FX 8.
Trains   7FX 9.
Wind   7FX10.
Fanfares   7FX21.

Miscellaneous
Industrial Engines, Argo EAF 140.
Real Plane Sounds, Saga ARC.
Real Train Sounds, Saga ARC.
Railroad Sounds, Transatlantic Records AFSD 5843.
The Sounds of Steam, Argo.
Giants of Steam, STO DFE 8536.

Churchbells, HMV EFX 110.
City Traffic and Transport, EFX 112 HMV.
Children, HMV EFX 116.
Sports and Spectacles, EFX 117.

Sounds of the Sea and Ships, Argo DA 37.

Sixty Years of Motoring, Argo ZN F2.

Railway Record, Argo EAF 135/136.

The Sounds and Songs of London, Columbia SAX 9001.
The Sounds of London, Sonologue, S.L. 101.

BBC recordings
Fun at the Zoo, Roundabout 1.
Animal Magic, Roundabout 4.
The End of Steam, REB 30M.
Powered Flight, REB 40M.
BBC Sound Effects, No. 1, RED 47M.
BBC Sound Effects, No. 2 RED 76M.
Highlights of 21 years of BBC Sports' Reports, REC 29M.
BBC Radiophonic Music, REC 25M.
Narrow Boats, REC 56M.
A Salute to Ludwig Koch, RED 34M.
British Mammals and Amphibians, RED 42M.
Cats and Dogs, RED 54M.
Sounds of the Countryside, RED 60M.
Highland Birds, RED 74M.
Wild Life of East Anglia, RED 83M.
Movement Mime and Music, RESR 5.

Listen, Move and Dance series
1. HMV 7 EG 8727
2. HMV 7 EG 8728
3. HMV 7 EG 8762
4. HMV CLP 3531.

Movement, Mime and Music, Paxton, E7p 315/316.
Music for two mimes (Down Our Street/Western Trail),
Paxton SLPT/1004.

Other material from Castle Effects Records, Recorded Tuition Ltd.,
174 Maybank Road, South Woodford, London, E.18.

Taped sounds from Sound Recordings, Shottery, Stratford on Avon.
(Specify tape recorder speed preferred — $3\frac{3}{4}$ or $7\frac{1}{2}$ i.p.s. — price
approx 60p for 30 to 60 seconds of sound).
Stage Sound (London) Ltd., 11–12 King Street, London, W.C.2.

Useful books

B.B.C. School Radio and the Tape Recorder (B.B.C.).
Jones, J. Graham: *Teaching With Tape* (The Focal Press).
Lloyd, Joseph M: *The All In One Tape Recorder Book* (The Focal Press).
Nijen, C. G: *The Tape Recorder* (Iliffe Books).
Sharp, P. E. M: *Sound and Vision* (Macdonald).
Wood, D. Neville: *On Tape — The Creative Use of the Tape Recorder*
(Ward Lock).
Woodman, H: *The Drama Tape Book* (Focal Press).

APPENDIX 2 VISION AND THE CELEBRATION

Mention is made in many of the celebrations of the use of projected pictures. There is much to commend the use of such aids because they do command attention and they do provide another very sophisticated dimension to the programme. Films, filmstrips and slides can be used prior to a festival to prepare the children. Too frequently we imagine that information and impressions of facts and details well known to us, are full and clear. Such a preliminary survey of the theme to be covered will ensure an informed, and we hope, enthusiastic group. This may well be more effective if taken in small groups.

Where projected aids are used during a celebration in the hall, a good blackout is necessary even when using a daylight projection screen. Adjustments to the curtains are best made before the festival begins or during an interval. Some of the film, or slides, etc., should be projected before the programme begins so that focusing, and volume (where appropriate) are adjusted. Where it is necessary to remove both the screen and the projector stand during the early part of the performance their positions should be marked on the floor. Spare fuses and projector lamps should be kept handy. Early booking of films is necessary to ensure that they will be available on the days required.

In the case of slides, their order should be decided upon and some mark made on each holder to ensure that each is the right way up. Where a number of people are involved, a rehearsal of that section of the programme is advisable with tape recorder, slide projector and announcer synchronising their activities.

An interesting technique of using two slide projectors is well described and illustrated in the free booklet *Notes on Photography* by A. Francombe, from Kodak Ltd., Kingsway, London, W.1. The projectors are linked, and focused on a single screen. A shutter device is fitted over each lens unit, so that by operating a lever, one picture, projected from one machine fades while the next slide, from the other machine comes sharply into focus. Since this system can be coupled with tape-recorded sound, a new dimension in aural and visual education is opened up.

USEFUL BOOKS
Hall, Knight, Hunt and Lovell: *Film Teaching* (B.F.L.).
Kidd, M. K. and Long, C. W: *Projecting Slides* (Focal Press).
Kingdom, J. M: *A Classified Guide to Sources of Educational Film Material* (N.C.A.V.A.E.).
Simpson, Margaret: *Film Projecting without tears and technicalities* (N.C.A.V.A.E.).
Still Photography in Education (N.C.A.V.A.E.).
Projecting Slides and Filmstrips (Kodak).

FILM LIBRARIES
Application should be made for catalogues and booking forms. Most will require an assurance that the projector is suitable for sound films and that a competent operator is available.
BBC Television Enterprises Film Hire
25 The Burroughs,
Hendon,
London, N.W.4.

British Transport Films,
Melbury House,
London, N.W.4.

Central Booking Agency (for registered members of the British Film Institute),
72 Dean Street,
London, W1V 6AA.

Central Film Library, Government Building,
Bromyard Avenue,
London, W.3.

Concord Films Council,
Nacton,
Ipswich, Suffolk.

Gas Council Film Library,
6-7 Great Chapel Street,
London, W1V 3AG.

Gateway Educational Films Ltd.,
470-472 Green Lanes,
Palmers Green,
London, N.13.

I.C.I. Film Library,
Thames House North,
Millbank,
London, S.W.1.

National Audio-Visual Aids Library
(for EFVA and NCAVAE films),
2 Paxton Place,
Gypsy Road,
London, S.E.27.

National Coal Board Film Library,
68-70 Wardour Street,
London, W1V 3HP.

Petroleum Films Bureau,
4 Brook Street,
Hanover Square,
London W1Y 2AY.

Rank Film Library,
P.O. Box 70, Great West Road,
Brentford, Middlesex.

Unilever Film Library,
Unilever House,
Blackfriars,
London, E.C.4.

Sound Services Ltd.,
Kingston Road,
Merton Park,
London, S.W.19.

Columbia Pictures Corporation Ltd.,
Film House,
142 Wardour Street,
London, W.1.

Connoisseur Films Ltd.,
167 Oxford Street,
London, W1R 2DX.

Contemporary Films Ltd.,
55 Greek Street,
London, W1V 6DB.

Film Distributors Associated (16mm) Ltd.,
(representing United Artists
and Twentieth-Century Fox),
37-41 Mortimer Street,
London, W1A 2JL.

Ron Harris Cinema Services Ltd.,
Glenbuck House,
Surbiton, Surrey.

Hunter Films Ltd.,
182 Wardour Street,
London, W1V 4BH.

Warner Pathé Distributors Ltd.,
135 Wardour Street,
London, W.1.

A number of educational authorities have a film library from which schools in their area can borrow, while others have favourable trading terms with the National Audio-Visual Aids Library.

Many embassies, consulates and commonwealth offices have film libraries illustrating features about their particular countries and application should be made to their PR department when the country is being featured in a celebration.

Certain professional and other organisations also maintain film collections usually about their sphere of activities but occasionally sponsoring some purely educational or informational enterprise. Details of many of these firms and their newest releases appear in the monthly magazine *Visual Education* from the National Committee for Audio-Visual Aids in Education (and in their frequently-revised catalogues of all such aids).

FILMS

Festival organisers will find it useful to examine the way in which others work. This is a list of films which feature particular events, high days and holidays in different parts of the world and illustrate the way in which people enjoy themselves in this special way.

Lord Siva Danced (Shell Films from Petroleum Films Bureau).
Martial Dances of Malabar (Shell Films from PFB).
Festival Log Book – survey of Motor Car Rallies (PFB).
Veterans of the Road (Esso Films).
The Royal Agricultural Show (Unilever).
Island of Surprise – featuring the Battle of the Flowers (Jersey
    Tourist Department, from Rank Films).
A Day at the Show (Norwich Union Insurance Society).
Festival Times (Holi, Goki Asthami, Garesh Chaturhi, Dassera and
    Divali – the most picturesque and widely celebrated festival –
    Public Relations Department, India House).
King Winter (The annual winter carnival at St. Paul's Minnesota –
    Rank Films).
A Christmas Play (Surrey Schools from Connoisseur Films).
Festival in Kano (Great Salla Festival which follows the Fast of
    Ramadhan – Gateway Films from Sound Services).
The Holland Festival (Phillips Electric from Sound Services).

184

The Circus (Fordson Newsreel No. 17 from Sound Services).

Jubilee Jamboree (about the great gathering of Scouts – Booke Bond Tea Co. from Sound Services).

The Golden Years (showing the annual festival of the orange harvest in Seville – James Robertson Ltd. from Sound Services).

Our Daily Bread (includes an unusual harvest festival – Sunblest Bakeries from Sound Services).

Siam (includes festival activities – Walt Disney Productions).

Alaskan Eskimo (includes celebration and feasting after the Time of Waiting has ended and the sun has returned – Walt Disney Productions).

Circus Art (BBC TV Enterprises).

Edinburgh (including the Festival and Tattoo – Campbell Harper Films).

Royal Tonga (a filmed record of all the ancient festivities of this island – BBC TV Enterprises).

People of the Skeena (life and celebrations on an Indian Reservation – National Film Board of Canada from Sound Services).

The Coronation of Richard III (study extract – Rank Films).

The Wedding Feast (parable from Matthew XXII – Religious Films Ltd.).

Primitive People (includes feasting and other ritual activities, e.g. The Corroboree – Rank Films).

Cinemagazine II (includes Thames race for Dogget's Coat and Badge – Petroleum Films Bureau).

Oil Review 12 (includes Emmett's Festival Railway – PFB).

Oil Review 15 (includes a Country Fair – PFB).

The Opening Ceremony of the House of Commons (EFVA).

The British Monarchy (EFVA).

The Coronation of Queen Elizabeth II (Rank Films).

A Queen is Crowned (Pathé).

Elizabeth is Queen (A.B. Pathé).

Royal Tour – Fiji and Tonga (A.B. Pathé).

Welcome the Queen (a triumphant return to London in 1954 – A.B. Pathé).

Holiday (British Transport Films).

One, Potato, Two Potato (British Film Institute).

The Singing Street (British Film Institute).

APPENDIX 3 BIBLIOGRAPHY AND DISCOGRAPHY

CELEBRATIONS, FESTIVALS AND OTHER EVENTS

Anglesey, Marchioness of: *The Countrywoman's Year* (Michael Joseph).

Bailey, Leslie: *BBC Scrap Books, Vol. I & II, 1896–1914* (Allen & Unwin).

Betts, John: *The Pageantry of London City* (Corporation of London).

Christian, Roy: *Old English Customs* (Country Life).

Cooper, Gordon: *Festivals of Europe* (Percival Marshall).

Farjeon, Eleanor: *A New Book of Days* (Oxford University Press).

Gascoigne, Margaret: *Discovering English Customs* (Shire Publications).

Frazer, Sir John: *The Golden Bough* (Macmillan).

Hill, Douglas: *Magic and Superstition* (Paul Hamlyn).

Howard, Alexander: *Endless Cavalcade* (Arthur Baker).

James, E. O: *Seasonal Feasts and Festivals* (Thames and Hudson).

Hunt, Cecil: *British Customs and Ceremonies* (Benn).

Mackie, Albert: *Scottish Pageantry* (Hutchinson).

Opie, I. & P: *The Lore and Language of School Children* (OUP).

Radford, E. & M. A: *Encyclopaedia of Superstitition* (Hutchinson).

Ritchie, James: *Singing Street* (Oliver and Boyd).

Smith, Alan: *Discovering Folklore in Industry* (Shire Publications).

Stoll, D. G: *Music Festivals of the World* (Pergamon).

Thonger, Richard: *A Calendar of German Customs* (Wolff).

Vipont, Elfrida: *Some Christian Festivals* (Michael Joseph).

Waters, Derek: *A Book of Festivals* (Mills and Boon).

Whistler, L: *The English Festivals* (Heinemann).

Wilcox, R. T: *Folk and Festival Customs of the World* (Batsford).

Anon: *Royal Pageantry* (Purnell).

Dictionary of Dates and Anniversaries (Newnes).

Whitaker's Almanack.

Calendar of Significant Dates (Allen and Unwin).

Coming Events – a monthly magazine from the British Travel Association.

SOURCE MATERIAL

Bates, E. and Bartless, P: *Impetus to Integrated Studies* (pupils' books, pictures, and teachers' book — Ginn).

Marshall, Sybil: *Expression* (Books 1–6 ,Rupert Hart Davis).

Pluckrose, Henry: *Creative Themes* (Evans).

Background pamphlets for many radio and TV programmes list poems, music, drama ideas, etc. ITV's series *Picture Box* compiled by Sybil Marshall is an excellent example.

Also BBC music, movement and mime and music workshop series.

POETRY

Some anthologies listed under the compiler or author.

Baldwin, Michael: *Poems by children* (Routledge and Kegan Paul).

Blishen, E: *The Oxford Book of Poetry* (Oxford).

Causley, Charles: *Rising Early* and *Dawn and Dusk* (Brockhampton).

Chisholm, E: *The Golden Staircase* (Nelson).

Clark, L: *Drums and Trumpets* (Bodley Head).

Gibson, J. and Wilson, R: *Rhyme and Rhythm* — 4 books (Macmillan).
　　　Much of the material is recorded on Argo records RG414/5/6/7.

Graham, E: *A Thread of Gold* (Bodley Head)
　　　A Puffin Quartet of Poets (Puffin).
　　　Puffin Book of Verse (Penguin).

Greaves, Margaret: *Scrap Box* (Methuen).

Grigson, G: *The Cherry Tree* (Phoenix).

Hodgart, Matthew: *Book of Ballads* (Faber).

Holbrook, D: *Iron, Honey, Gold* — Vols. 1, 2, 3 & 4 (Cambridge).

Ireson, Barbara: *Come to the Fair* (Faber).

Kirkup, James: *Shepherding Winds* (Blackie).

Mackay, David: *A Flock of Words* (Bodley Head).

Parry, H: *The Merry Minstrel* (Blackie).

Reeves, J: *The Merry-Go-Round* (Heinemann).

Saunders, Ruth Manning: *A Bundle of Ballads* (Oxford).

Smith, J: *My Kind of Verse* (Burke).

Stevenson, R. L: *A Child's Garden of Verses* (Oxford).

Summerfield, Geoffrey: *Voices* — 3 volumes (Penguin).
　　　Junior Voices — 4 volumes (Penguin).

Taconis, Liba: *Lean out of the Window* (Blackwell).

Whitlocks, P: *All Day Long* (Oxford).

White, Tessa: *Visual Poetry for Creative Expression* (Macdonald & Evans).

Withers, Carl: *A Rocket in my Pocket* (Bodley Head).
Wollman, Maurice and Grugeon, David: *Happenings* (Harrap).
Woodland, E. J. M: *Poems for Movement* (Evans).

Come Follow Me (Evans).
Comic and Curious Verse (Penguin)
More Comic and Curious Verse (Penguin).

POETRY ANTHOLOGIES ON RECORD
Age groupings are suggested by recording companies.

Searching Years – Poetry and Music, Abbey MVP/635/636/637
    (for age groups 8-11, 11-14, 14 plus).
Poetry and Song Argo DA 50-52 (Book 1 – Macmillan 12-13 years).
              Argo 53, 54, 55 (Book 2 – Macmillan 13-14 years).
              Argo 56, 57, 58, 59 (Book 3 – Macmillan 14-15 years).
              Argo 60, 61, 62, 63 (Book 4 – Macmillan 15-16 years).
Anthology of English Verse, Jupiter jun00B 1/3/5/7.
Book of Ballads, Jupiter jur 00A3 (Junior and Secondary).
A World of Searching Eyes, Abbey VP 631/2.
Favourite Poems, read by Robert Donat, Argo RG 192.
Choral Verse, Oliver and Boyd, OBEP 101A (7-11 years).
Happenings, Harrap Audio-Visual Aids Ltd. (9-13 years).
              (*Happenings*, a book of poems, Harrap.)
The Jupiter Anthology of 20th-century English Poetry, Jupiter,
    JUR 00A1/2 (13-18 years).
Nonsense Verse, Caedmon TC 1078 (secondary).
Palgrave's Golden Treasury, Caedmon TC 0998/9 (secondary).
The Pattern of Poetry, HMV CLP 1724 (junior and secondary).
Poems and Songs for Younger Children, Jupiter JEP OC 30/OC11
    (7-11 years).
Poems of Childhood, Argo EAF 108 (junior and secondary).
Poems of Nature, Argo EAF 104 (junior and secondary).
Rhyme and Rhythm, Argo 414/5/6/7 (7-11 years – series of books
    published by Macmillan).
The Voice of Poetry, Columbia DB188 (secondary).
Wallace's Private Zoo, Parlaphone GE 18581.
Poems of the Sea, Argo EAF 90 (junior and secondary).
Poems of Voyaging and Discovery, Argo EAF 106 (junior and secondary).
Golden Treasury of American Verse, Spoken Arts 772.

WRITING

Dean, Joan: *Reading, Writing and Talking* (Black).

    Children Writing (Berkshire County Council).

Druce, Robert: *The Eye of Innocence* (Brockhampton Press).

Ford, B: *Young Writers, Young Readers* (Hutchinson).

Holbrook, David: *Children Writing* (Cambridge University Press).

Hound, M. L. and Cooper, G. E: *Coming into their own* (Heinemann).

Lane, S. M. and Kemp, B: *An Approach to Creative Writing in the Primary School* (Blackie).

Langdon, Margaret: *Let The Children Write* (Longmans).

Maybury, Barry: *Creative Writing for Juniors* (Batsford).

Peel, M: *Seeing To The Heart* (Chatto and Windus).

Pym, Dora: *Free Writing* (University of London Press).

West Riding County Council: *The Excitement of Writing* (Chatto & Windus).

Whitehead, Frank: *Disappearing Dias* (Chatto & Windus).

DRAMA AND MOVEMENT

Allen, John: *Drama* (HMSO).

Beresford, Margaret: *How To Make Puppets and Teach Puppetry* (Mills and Boon).

Billing, R. N., Pemberton and Clegg, J. D: *Teaching Drama* (ULP).

Barr, Enid: *From Story into Drama* (Heinemann).

Bruce, V: *Dance and Dance Drama in Education* (Pergamon).

Carnie, Winifred M: *Listening and Moving* (Nelson).

Haggerty, Joan: *Please Miss, Can I Play God?* (Methuen).

Haskell, Arnold: *The Story of Dance* (Rathbone).

Hodgson, John and Richards, Ernest: *Improvisation* (Methuen).

James, Ronald: *Infant Drama* (Nelson).

Kennedy, Douglas: *English Folk Dancing* (Arco).

Martin, William and Vallins, Gordon: *Exploration Drama* with books — Carnival, Legend, Horizon and Routes (Evans).

Morgan, Elizabeth: *A Practical Guide to Drama in the Primary School* (Ward Lock).

Nuttall, Kenneth: *Your Book of Acting* (Faber).

Robinson, Stuart: *Exploring Puppetry* (Mills and Boon).

Russell, Joan: *Creative Dance in the Primary School* (Macdonald & Evans).

Sharp, Cecil: *The Country Dance Book* — 6 parts (Novello).

Slade, Peter: *An Introduction to Child Drama* (ULP).

    Child Drama (ULP).

Snook, Barbara: *Fancy Dress for Children* (Batsford).

        Costumes for School Plays (Batsford).

Way, Brian: *Development Through Drama* (Longmans).

Williams, Iolo A: *English Folk Song and Dance* (Longmans).

ART AND CRAFT

Alexander, Eugenie: *Fabric Pictures* (Mills and Boon).

Andrew, Laye: *Creative Rubbings* (Batsford).

d'Arbeloff, Natalie and Yates, Jack: *Creating in Collage* (Studio Vista).

Aspen, George: *Modelmaking in Paper, Board and Metal* (Studio Vista).

Eves, John: *Modelmaking in Schools*.

Grater, Michael: *Make it in Paper* (Mills and Boon).

        One Piece of Paper (Mills and Boon).

        Paper Faces (Mills and Boon).

        Paper People (Mills and Boon).

Green, Peter: *Introducing Surface Painting* (Mills and Boon).

Hart, Tony: *The Young Designer* (Kaye and Ward).

Hartung, Rolph: *Creative Textile Crafts* (Batsford).

Honda, Isao: *How to Make Oragami* (Museum Press).

Johnson, Pauline: *Creating With Paper* (Kaye).

Kinsey, A: *Simple Screen Printing* (Dryad).

Maile, Anne: *Tie and Dye as a Present Day Craft* (Mills and Boon).

        Tie and Dye made easy (Mills and Boon).

Melzi, Kay: *Art in the Primary School* (Blackwell).

Moorey, Anne and Christopher: *Making Mobiles* (Studio Vista).

Pluckrose, Henry: *Let's Make Pictures* (Mills and Boon).

        Let's Work Large (Mills and Boon).

        Creative Arts and Crafts (Oldbourne).

        Introducing Crayon Techniques (Batsford).

Proud, Nora: *Textile Printing and Dyeing* (Batsford).

Rottger, Ernst: *Creative Wood Craft* (Batsford).

        Creative Clay Craft (Batsford).

        Creative Paper Craft (Batsford).

Sandford, Lettice and Davis, Philla: *Decorative Straw Work* (Batsford).

Seyd, Marie: *Designing with String* (Batsford).

Slade, Richard: *Masks and How To Make Them* (Faber).

Snook, Barbara: *Making Clowns, Witches and Dragons* (Batsford).

Tritton, Gottfried: *Art Techniques for Children* (Batsford).

Waters, Derek: *Creative Work with Found Materials* (Mills and Boon).

Weiss, Harvey: *The Young Sculptor* (Nicholas Kaye).

        The Young Print Maker (Nicholas Kaye).

Zanker, Francis O: *Foundations of Design in Wood* (Dryad).

EXCURSIONS AND FIELDWORK

Arcgerm, J. E. and Dalton, T. H: *Fieldwork in Geography* (Batsford).

Anderson, M. D: *History By The Highway* (Faber).

Dilke, M. S: *Field Work for Schools* – Vol. 1 (Rivingtons).

Douch, Robert: *Local History and the Teacher* (Routledge & Kegan Paul).

Fisher, James: *Shell Nature Lover's Atlas* (Ebury Press and Michael Joseph).

Ford, V. E: *How To Begin Your Fieldwork* – *Seashore* (Murray).
Woodland (Murray).

Hammersley, A. and others: *Approaches to Environmental Studies* (Blandford).

Harrison, Molly: *Changing Museums* (Longmans).
Learning Out Of School (Ward, Lock Educational).

Hoskins, W. G: *Fieldwork in Local History* (Faber).

Sauvain, B: *Exploring at Home* (Hulton).

The Treasures of Britain (Drive Publications Ltd.).

Museums and Galleries (Index Publishers).

Historic Houses and Castles (Index Publishers).

Visitor's London and many leaflets (London Transport).

I-Spy Books (The Dickens Press).

Discovering Series (Shire Publications).

MUSIC

Buck, Percy: *The Oxford Nursery Song Book* (Oxford).

Fiske, Roger and Dobbs, J. P. B: *The Oxford Music Books* 1-4 (OUP).

Hitchcock, Gordon: *The Song Tree* (Curwen).
The Song Fair (Curwen).

Hugill, Stanley: *Shanties of the Seven Seas* (Routledge and Kegan Paul).

Reynolds, G: *A European Folk Song Book* (Boosey and Hawkes).
Folk Songs of France (Boosey and Hawkes).

Sharp, Cecil and Karpels, Maud: *Eighty English Folk Songs* (Faber).

Seegar, Ruth Crawford: *American Folk Songs for Children* (Doubleday, New York).

Smith, Peter: *Faith, Folk and Clarity* (Galliard).
Faith, Folk and Nativity (Galliard).
Faith, Folk and Festivity (Galliard).

Warwick, Alan R: *A Noise of Music* (Queen Anne Press).

Williams, Vaughan and Lloyd: *The Penguin Books of Folk Songs* (Penguin).

RECORDS

Oats and Beans and Barley (Argo ZDA44).

Songs for Singing Children (EMI XLP 50008).

Gospel Songs for Little Children (EMI MFP 1350).

Let's Make Music (CLP 3649).

Come Listen (EMI MFP 1349 – with an accompanying book by Ian Campbell – Ginn).

Youth Sings (EMI CSD 3640).

The Spinner's Clockwork Story Book (Fontana SFL 13191).

Ahmet the Woodseller, Meet My Folks (EMI XLP 40001).

The Midnight Thief (EMI DLP 1216).

The Aviary and The Insect World (EMI 7 EG 8943).

The Happy Prince (Argo ZNF 5).

The Carnival of the Animals (HMV 7 EG 134).

Children's Song Book (EMI MFP 1367).